STORM
THE
BALLOT
BOX

STORM THE BALLOT BOX

An Insider's Guide to a Voting Revolution

JO-ANN ROBERTS

NIMBUS
PUBLISHING
—— NIMBUS.CA ——

Do you want to know why there is such widespread public cynicism or apathy about politics and politicians? It's a rough, nasty game that shows how ideals are quickly overridden or compromised by the power of money, personality, and hidden agendas. Jo-Ann Roberts's *Storm the Ballot Box* offers important insights into how we can fix our broken electoral structures so every Canadian's voice is heard. This is not a cry to overthrow our current democratic order, but a plea for greater thought and involvement by civil society to get the changes needed.

DR. DAVID SUZUKI
author, geneticist, broadcaster

Part political catharsis, part urgent call to action, *Storm the Ballot Box* delivers a passionate argument for democratic reform in Canada. With a clear and engaging writing style, Jo-Ann Roberts makes complex political issues accessible, offering readers a thought-provoking examination of the deep-rooted challenges facing Canadian electoral politics today. Whether you're deeply concerned about the state of our political system or simply curious about the way forward, this book will resonate with anyone passionate about the future of Canadian democracy.

ALEX MARLAND
author and Jarislowsky Chair in Trust and
Political Leadership, Acadia University

Nimbus Publishing Limited
3660 Strawberry Hill Street, Halifax, NS, B3K 5A9
(902) 455-4286 nimbus.ca

Nimbus Publishing is based in Kjipuktuk, Mi'kma'ki, the traditional territory of the Mi'kmaq People.

No part of this book may be used in the training of generative artificial intelligence technologies or systems.

Printed and bound in Canada
NB1771

Editor: Angela Mombourquette
Cover & Interior Design: Bee Stanton

Library and Archives Canada Cataloguing in Publication

Title: Storm the ballot box : an insider's guide to a voting revolution / Jo-Ann Roberts ; foreword by the Right Honourable Kim Campbell.
Names: Roberts, Jo-Ann, author.
Description: Includes bibliographical references.
Identifiers: Canadiana (print) 20240492684 | Canadiana (ebook) 20240492714 | ISBN 9781774714355 (softcover) | ISBN 9781774714362 (EPUB)
Subjects: LCSH: Voting—Canada.
Classification: LCC JL193 .R63 2025 | DDC 324.60971—dc23

Nimbus Publishing acknowledges the financial support for its publishing activities from the Government of Canada, the Canada Council for the Arts, and from the Province of Nova Scotia. We are pleased to work in partnership with the Province of Nova Scotia to develop and promote our creative industries for the benefit of all Nova Scotians.

For Georgia, Mae, Miles, and Miguel—
the next generation of voters.

CONTENTS

A PHILOSOPHER FRIEND USED TO SAY, "THE UNIT OF human understanding is the story."

In writing *Storm the Ballot Box: An Insider's Guide to a Voting Revolution*, Jo-Ann Roberts tells her story of involvement with the Canadian political system as journalist, candidate, party leader, and campaign manager. Her journalistic skills make the story lively and interesting.

Roberts sets out to identify weaknesses in our current practice of politics in Canada—concluding with a list of recommendations for action. From the perspective of my own story, I found many of her arguments pertinent—often addressing overlooked issues.

Among the issues she identifies that do not always get attention are the pitfalls of public opinion polling. She relates these to what she describes as the perils of so-called "strategic voting," but she identifies a phenomenon that appeared in the 2016 Trump–Clinton US election—that is, misleading polls that overstate or understate support for a candidate or a party. She argues that the margin of error of a poll is critical to assessing what weight to give it, but that this is rarely discussed fully in the press treatment of polling. The differences between polls and their reliability are a direct reflection of who is doing the polling. As seen recently in the

US, there are numerous right-wing polling organizations whose purpose is to achieve results that favour Republicans. For some reason, the political left has not engaged in this activity to nearly the same degree. There are polling organizations whose results are considered sound by polling experts based on their methodology—sample size, method of contact, and calculation of the margin of error. Roberts's recommendation that Elections Canada limit the margin of error of polls released during a campaign is an interesting response to misleading polls.

The voting public would benefit enormously from better coverage of polling per se, not just the results of polls, but Roberts argues further that polling leads to strategic voting, which she regards as a trap. As a candidate for the Green Party, Roberts learned that many constituents who regarded her as the best candidate on a personal basis would nonetheless not vote for her because her party could not form a government. While I sympathize with her frustration, I think strategic voting is essential and that all votes should be cast strategically. If that means that worthy candidates who would otherwise gain support do not, the remedy is in the structure and rules of the political process.

Roberts speaks eloquently about the alternatives to our "first-past-the-post" system in Canada, which works to the disadvantage of small political parties. In a parliamentary system where there is no separation of powers, but, rather, where the Executive is created out of the legislature, support for smaller parties can divide the vote in a way that allows a party less representative of the popular consensus to form a government. For example, in my view, the most important issue facing us today is climate change. (I sit on the Climate Overshoot Commission, a group of independent global leaders who have built a strategy to mitigate risks should

*Broadcaster
Jo-Ann Roberts
interviews former
prime minister
Kim Campbell
in Victoria, BC,
on June 7, 2008.*
[KEN KELLY]

global warming exceed established targets.) For me, to vote for a
party that is committed to climate action but that I know will not
form a government and, therefore, not set the agenda, runs the risk
of allowing a climate change–denying party to form a government
by splitting the climate-action vote. In 2021, the Liberals formed a
minority government with the support of the NDP, which allowed
them to pursue a climate-action agenda. Small parties can use their
small caucuses to bolster the support of like-minded parties who
are able to form a government, but that is risky. So if we want to
give more voice to smaller parties to reflect the views of their supporters more strongly, we need to look at how we vote and allocate
power among parties in Parliament.

On these issues, Roberts is very interesting and presents a
number of different voting systems that could address her concerns. Alas, changes are easier said than done. In British Columbia,
the Social Credit Party under W. A. C. Bennett won seven consecutive elections from 1952 to 1972. The first was as a minority government, then, with a single transferable vote (STV) election, they
won a majority. After that election, they returned to the first-past-
the-post system. Prime Minister Justin Trudeau promised after his

election that it would be the last federal election fought under the first-past-the-post system. He said it would be replaced by a form of proportional representation. That change has yet to happen. Roberts discusses the many commissions on electoral reform and their recommendations, but laments that no change is in the offing.

Proportional representation is not without its own problems. In some countries, such as Israel, a multitude of parties with narrow platforms can result in coalitions that give disproportionate power to extremist parties. My own view is that single transferable vote or "runoff"systems (as in France) can address some of the issues that Roberts identifies without creating instability. What is important about her discussion is that she identifies a key issue that needs to be addressed.

Storm the Ballot Box includes thoughtful discussions of many other issues that could contribute to better voter information, higher voter turnout, and fairer financing of political campaigns. Woven through all these discussions is Roberts's passion for the democratic electoral process, a passion which I share. As the daughter of two Second World War veterans, I have always been aware of the price Canadians have paid to defend democracy both at home and abroad. Younger generations may not have the same historical referents to put the privilege and duty of voting in context. Roberts's fifth chapter, "Future Present: On the Importance of Raising Young Voters," is particularly apt today.

A short foreword is no substitute for diving into this informative book. For anyone interested in understanding and improving democratic political life in Canada, this is an excellent resource. It deserves wide readership.

– Rt. Hon. A. Kim Campbell
19th Prime Minister of Canada

INTRODUCTION

POLITICS MATTERS

I REMEMBER WHEN I DISCOVERED THAT POLITICS MATTERED. It was 1966. I was ten years old, going into grade 5. I had long, straight hair parted in the middle. I liked the Monkees and collecting Beatles cards. I shared a room with Laurie, my younger sister. My brother, David, was five and had his own room. My best friend Heather and I would have weekend sleepovers and complain about our little brothers and sisters, talk about teachers, and dream about what it would be like to have a Princess phone in our rooms someday.

I adored my dad. He was so smart. As a United Church minister in a small New Brunswick town, he was someone people listened to and respected. He spent Saturday nights in his study with his books around him, practising his sermons. On Saturday afternoons, when my mom was pregnant with my sister Jane, Dad and I usually went grocery shopping. Dad said getting the groceries was our way of helping. It made me feel special to have Dad all to myself as we pushed the cart around the IGA and picked up the things Mom had put on the list—spaghetti sauce, butter, cornflakes, and

Dad's favourite cookies: chocolate marshmallow puffs. We also bought Carnation powdered milk so we could make our skim milk every night. We didn't have much money, so we had to be careful at the grocery store. Occasionally we got to the checkout and didn't have enough cash, and I always wanted to disappear from embarrassment. Fortunately, Dad was so well known the store manager always said, "Don't worry, Bruce. Just drop by tomorrow with the money." And he always did.

I sometimes wonder what those conversations were like when we got home. I never really thought of us as poor. We lived in a nice house—a manse provided by the church. Mom looked after the finances. We drove a nice car because Dad knew the car dealer and he always gave us a good deal.

A Roberts family photo taken in Fredericton, NB, in December 1966. Standing: Roberts's brother, David, and her father, Bruce Roberts. Seated, from L: Jo-Ann Roberts, her sister Laurie, and her mother, Ella (holding baby Jane).
[AUTHOR COLLECTION]

Mom was beautiful and loved being a mother. She and Dad were crazy about each other, and, even without much money, life was good.

We lived in Nashwaaksis, NB, a small town across the river from the provincial capital of Fredericton. Politics was always the talk of the town. Louis Robichaud was the premier. "P'tit-Louis," as he was known, was the first Acadian to be elected premier of New Brunswick. My Dad, who was a Newfoundlander, was a big fan of P'tit-Louis.

Louis Robichaud was a Liberal, but it wasn't his party affiliation that impressed my dad. Dad admired Robichaud's policies—policies that levelled the playing field for Acadians in New Brunswick. His signature initiative was called "Equal Opportunity." It changed the tax system so schools were equally funded in all areas of the province, allowing economically disadvantaged French communities to provide the same quality of education as wealthier English communities.

Dad would have political conversations with friends when we were in the grocery store. Equal Opportunity was very controversial, and those conversations were often lively. In the car on the drive home, we would talk about how P'tit-Louis was making a real difference in the lives of people like us who lived in other parts of the province. Dad even mentioned it in a sermon one Sunday. That didn't go over very well with some members of the congregation. I remember eavesdropping on my parents when they were talking about the situation; I think Dad's job was on the line. Dad said he felt he had no choice—this was a question of justice.

I was fascinated. Politicians could make a difference, and politics mattered to grown-ups.

The following year, I decided to run for president of our grade 6 class's Red Cross Society—and won. My surprised teacher told me she didn't think I should have won because I didn't understand how to run a Red Cross meeting. (In retrospect, she'd clearly had a favourite in the race, and it wasn't me.) Her words spurred me to act. I went home and devoured *Robert's Rules of Order*.

My dad and I went on to have hundreds of political debates over the years. Sometimes we agreed and sometimes we didn't, but one thing I know is that my parents raised an engaged and committed voter.

When I was young, it seemed to me that everyone voted, even if not everyone talked about politics. The numbers support this. In the 1960s, '70s, and '80s, voter turnout in Canada was between 75 and

80 percent. Since then, it has dropped to between 60 and 70 percent. We know this is happening, but we are not talking about why it's happening. We also don't seem to be doing anything to fix it.

This book doesn't have all the answers; it does raise a lot of questions. My hope is that it will start a revolution of sorts—a voting revolution. I have a lot of ideas about how to improve our democracy and how to make changes that will get more people engaged with our democracy, and I'm not alone in this quest. I have been inspired by books like *Teardown: Rebuilding Democracy from the Ground Up* by Dave Meslin, and by people like Green Party co-leader Elizabeth May, senators like the late Hugh Segal and Marilou McPhedran, and author David Moscrop (*Too Dumb for Democracy? Why We Make Bad Political Decisions and How We Can Make Better Ones*).

Fair Vote Canada (a national citizens' campaign that "recognizes proportional representation as the most fundamental and urgent change needed in Canadian politics") and the Samara Centre for Democracy (a non-partisan organization whose "vision is a resilient democracy with responsive institutions, shaped by an engaged public") are making the case for a better voting system.

This book aims to get Canadians to vote, no matter who they vote for.

—————

I've been a Green Party candidate four times in my life. I was interim leader of the Green Party of Canada from November 2019 to October 2020 and deputy leader of the Green Party of Nova Scotia from 2021 to 2024. A reporter recently asked me, "Why do you think the Greens are having so much trouble getting elected now that climate change seems to be important to voters?"

It's a good question. I think the reporter was hoping I would blame internal conflicts within the federal Green Party. It's true that internal conflicts can wreak havoc inside a political party, but the Greens are not the only party to have discovered this. Even a party that is in power can become divided when it starts to lose at the polls. The Liberals, the Conservatives, and the New Democrats have all seen this happen.

When I first entered the political ring, I asked myself the same question posed by the reporter. Why aren't there more Greens in the House of Commons and in our provincial legislatures?

The answer seemed simple: our electoral system was created for a two-party system, and that needs to change. My next question for myself was—so why doesn't it change? This book grew out of those questions.

I want *Storm the Ballot Box* to be a rallying cry. I want every eligible Canadian to vote in every election for all orders of government—federal, provincial, and municipal. I truly believe that if we can get people to vote, we can get them to care, leading to even more engagement. It doesn't mean we shouldn't keep working to improve the system to make it more meaningful and to build other forms of democracy, but voting is simple and effective, and it's a good place to start.

I always thought I would study law and probably work in government or enter politics. I was progressive but not partisan. My family knew politicians of all political stripes, and I was encouraged to vote based on my principles. I studied political science in university and was a champion debater. My debating partner went on to a law degree, but in 1977, my last year of university, I decided I wanted to pursue journalism. I wanted to report on politics; I would fight for justice with a microphone.

This was the era of Watergate in the US; Woodward and Bernstein had exposed a scandal that brought down a president. Barbara Frum hosted *As It Happens* on CBC Radio and held world leaders and Canadian politicians accountable. It sounded exciting, and I wanted to be part of the action. I set my sights on working for the CBC, and though it wasn't a straight road, it did happen.

For nearly forty years I covered politics at all levels with a notebook, a tape recorder, a camera, or a studio microphone. I hosted election specials and investigated political rumours, and I thought I had a strong understanding of how our democracy worked.

Then, in 2014, things started to change. The CBC had been under attack by both Liberal and Conservative governments, but the government in power wanted to eliminate the public broadcaster in Canada. I wanted to fight that move. It was time to get political, and I couldn't do that while working at the CBC. I had prided myself on maintaining a non-partisan position as a journalist. I had consistently voted, but my political preferences were never known outside the voting booth.

I ran as a candidate in Victoria, BC, in the 2015 election for the Green Party of Canada. It was the beginning of my discovery of the other side of politics—what I hadn't known as a student or as a journalist. I went from the newsrooms into the backrooms, from one side of the microphone to the other. It was eye-opening, and it brought my view of our democracy into a whole new light.

After 2015 I joked that, if I ever got a tattoo, it would simply be the number 23,666—the number of people who voted for me in Victoria that year. I am grateful to every one of those voters. I didn't win; I came second, and I was devastated, but I had earned more votes than 131 of the MPs elected—more votes than Thomas

Mulcair, the leader of the NDP. But it didn't matter. Close only counts in horseshoes.

I've since run in two more federal elections and one provincial election; in total for all four elections, 33,009 people have voted for me. It's a humbling number. It also represents a lot of work—meeting those citizens and convincing them to vote. I am grateful to every one of them. And while I've never been a winner, I believe we can't give up on democracy.

We can do better if we know what's wrong. I don't have all the answers, but I do have some of them. I have stories that I think will get us talking about why millions of Canadians are not voting.

That is one reason I'm writing this book. I am also writing it for the generation of youth who are struggling with eco-anxiety. I want them to know that, while it's essential to take their issues to the street, they must also take them to the ballot box. If the voting system is letting them down, they need to get more people involved and change it.

I am writing this book for my grandchildren. I want them to know that democracy is worth fighting for, and I want my experience to have some value, although I worry that I haven't started early enough to fight for a better future for them. I hope this book will help them, their parents, and all those who are now taking on the challenge of creating a better democracy and a better world.

Readers don't have to agree with everything in this book. It's a slice in time and just one person's point of view, but it's a rare view—that of someone who is not in power, who has seen democracy at work from the inside, but who is not on the inside. Democracy needs critical thinking and healthy, respectful debate. I hope there's a ten-year-old girl out there, grocery shopping with a parent, who will benefit from overhearing a conversation about why it's important to vote. I hope she hears about someone making a difference in the world and decides that politics is interesting and important. I hope she promises herself that one day she'll be prime minister.

Let's start a revolution to protect democracy and make it stronger. Let's educate ourselves to create change—and then let's storm the ballot box.

CHAPTER 1

SCANDALMONGERING AND STRATEGIC VOTING

The Rise of the Muckraker

I T'S 6:00 A.M. ON SEPTEMBER 29, 2015, AND CHERYL THOMAS is fast asleep alone in her condo in Victoria, BC, when her phone rings. Six in the morning is never a good time to get a phone call. Her first thought is "something's happened." She answers, still groggy.

By the time she hangs up, the Liberal candidate for Victoria is in shock. Her world is spiralling out of control. The call wasn't from the police or a hospital; her dad, children, and grandchildren are all fine, but she is in tears.

"What's with the Black Santa?" the caller—a Liberal Party strategist—had asked.

It's dawn in Victoria, but the day is well under way in Ottawa, where it's 9:00 A.M. The *True North Times* (*TNT*), a satirical political news website, has just announced Cheryl Thomas as the ninth candidate in its "Nine Days of Scandal" series. The Liberal Party's war room has seen the post, and the word has gone out to party strategists in Vancouver: "Deal with it."

TNT has posted several of Thomas's Facebook posts in which she made statements that criticized Israel's treatment of Palestinians, saying, "Yes, hundreds of years ago the mosques were used as gathering places for education. Unfortunately, now the mosques are used as brainwashing stations, desecrating those holy places." She also posted a joke about why Santa is depicted as white: "You can't have a brown guy with a beard sneaking into your house in the middle of the night! You'd be calling the bomb squad!"

Political dynamite.

Cheryl Thomas's Facebook post, July 10, 2014, 1:45am (unedited)

Cheryl Thomas: Bob and Babak, one thing I learned in the Middle East is that we were fed the Israeli/British/American version of the conflict our whole lives - "the poor Israelis trying to build communes in the desert being attacked by those awful Arabs from all sides". And, I believed it. Then, I met some Palestinians whose families had been olive farmers for generations. They were physically removed from their homes and given no relocation compensation or anything. Their whole families scattered across the Middle East (and Europe and North America). They are now in their 60s and are "stateless. They have no home to go to. The oppressed of the Warsaw ghettos and the concentration camps have become the oppressors, keeping the Palestinians who are left in their homeland in ghettos where they limit their access to education and stop most opportunities for them to make a living. When unemployed young men fight back with rocks and crappy rockets, the Israelis blow the shit out of their neighborhoods, killing women and young children (collateral damage). Take a look at all the 'mini-wars' in the last decade; compare the Israeli deaths to the Palestinian/Lebanese/Egyptian deaths. Regardless of what agreements are negotiated over the last several decades, the fundamentalist Jews continue to illegally take more and more Palestinian land and "settle' there, continuing to displace Palestinians because they believe they have the 'right over all the lands. I could go on and on......"m just saying be open to the fact that there ARE two sides and unfortunately, we in the west have been fed only one side.

"I didn't even know what they were talking about. This was stuff from years ago," Thomas later told me in an interview. "I couldn't even think. All [the caller] said was, 'Tools down. Don't talk to the media.' I didn't call my campaign manager or my team. That was a mistake."

It's too late for the party to get Thomas's name off the ballot. The story appears on September 30, two days after the deadline for a candidate to be replaced. "The boys from Vancouver" tell her the party will put out a statement saying she is resigning from the race; her campaign office will be closed, and she will make no more public appearances or speak to the media.

Thomas, who teaches business at the University of Victoria, is crushed. She isn't new to politics, but this is her first time as a candidate. She has worked in the trenches for the Liberal Party, both provincially and federally, for over twenty years.

Thomas has been actively campaigning in the bucolic riding by the sea for over two months, since Prime Minister Stephen Harper dropped the writ to start the election at the beginning of August. She's raised money, knocked on doors, and participated in nearly a dozen debates. The Liberals are running third, with 90,000 voters in the riding. But the party's internal polling is showing a shift in the Liberals' favour growing across the country, and her numbers have been picking up in Victoria.

"Not enough to win. It was going to be an uphill battle to beat Murray," she said.

"Murray" refers to Murray Rankin—the incumbent. He won the riding in a by-election, narrowly defeating the Green Party candidate by a few hundred votes. He's a balding redhead; an affable lawyer who specializes in environmental law. He rides a bike, and during this campaign, he's never missed an event. He's good with names and is effective on the doorstep. The NDP believes keeping this seat out of the hands of the Greens is key to maintaining its strength on Vancouver Island.

Me? I am the Green Party candidate. According to the polls, I'm running a close second to the NDP. Thomas and Rankin like to call me the "celebrity radio host" in a tone that suggests that's not a good thing for someone who wants to be an MP. I've hosted the afternoon show on CBC Radio, *All Points West*, for the past ten years. I have covered politics and elections in several provinces since 1980 and, just eighteen months before the election, I won a fellowship to teach journalism at the University of Victoria.

I know the riding. At the CBC, I attended more than fifty public appearances a year for non-profit events. I'm keen, and I believe I can win this race. But, in reality, I'm about to learn about politics from the inside, and I will be shocked by what I don't know.

While Thomas grapples with the news that the Liberal Party has decided her political career is over, Murray Rankin and I are unaware that the race is about to change.

The Liberal Party campaign team, with just twenty days left until the election, doesn't want anything to stop the wave they see growing. Cheryl Thomas is told she has to drop out of the race because the party doesn't want anything to "distract" from the larger success they sense is coming their way.

She is a good party soldier and does what she is told. She signs off on a release apologizing for the Facebook posts. Later that night, she meets with her campaign team, locks her office, and leaves for Alberta, where she spends the rest of the election with her family.

"Nine Days of Scandal" was a creation of *True North Times* (*TNT*), a website run by five McGill students. Its initials are likely intentional, given that it blew up several political careers.

Back in 2013, there was a lot of grumbling about the changing nature of politics in Canada.

Jo-Ann Roberts prepares for a debate during the 2015 election in Victoria, BC, September 27, 2015, before Cheryl Thomas is forced to drop out of the race. L–R: Jo-Ann Roberts, Cheryl Thomas, Murray Rankin. [KEN KELLY]

Conservative party leader Stephen Harper was the prime minister, and everyone interested in politics was speculating about what could happen in the election in the fall of 2015.

Simren Sandhu, a writer and comedian who lived in Montréal, was a fan of *The Daily Show* with Jon Stewart and *Last Week Tonight* with John Oliver. Sandhu called his friend Daniel Etcovitch, who was studying at McGill. Sandhu told Etcovitch he had a vision: it was time to make Canadian politics more interesting by making it more fun. He said people their age found Canadian politics boring. He wanted to change that.

Next, Sandhu had called friend and fellow Montréaler Max Seltzer, who was also interested in politics. These young political junkies began to meet up regularly at their apartments in the off-campus home of hundreds of students, Le Plateau, which featured blonde brick buildings with black wrought iron steps and railings, high-rise apartment towers, dépanneurs, Indian and Asian takeout restaurants, and bustling bus stops.

It was here, over beer and pizza, that *TNT* was born.

A few other people joined the group but didn't stay. Sandhu, Etcovitch, and Seltzer were committed to making their idea a reality. They had decided Canada needed the kind of political satire that was readily available in US and the UK.

"Canada didn't have a culture of that, and we saw an opening," Etcovitch told me when I interviewed him a few years later. Initially, the guys wanted to start a television show. They pitched one, but it didn't fly, so in 2014 they launched a website: *True North Times*, "Real news—just funnier." The website says the creators' goal was not only to make Canadian politics accessible, but "to make it funny, to make it entertaining." Sandhu was president and CEO, Daniel Etcovitch was chief marketing officer and strategy officer, and Max Seltzer was chief operating officer and editor-in-chief.

The site attracted some initial attention from political parties and the media, but it didn't hit the big time until it launched "Nine Days of Scandal."

In August 2015, Sandhu, Seltzer, and Etcovitch set up the stories that would be part of "Nine Days of Scandal." They made sure they had their facts checked and double-checked. They were ready to go. With one click of a mouse, the page would go live. There was to be a new post on the website under the "Nine Days of Scandal" banner every day at the same time for the next nine days. At that point, Etcovitch headed off to study Law at Harvard. Seltzer and Sandhu held down the fort with a small crew. It was agreed that Etcovitch would handle media inquiries from Cambridge, Massachusetts, if needed.

"We want to bring the absurdity together in one place, comment on it and make you laugh," read the website.

On September 22, 2015, they hit "post."

It was not a laughing matter if you were one of the nine candidates targeted by *TNT*. Four were Liberals, two were Conservatives, and three were New Democrats. One went on to win his seat, two withdrew, and six lost.

We know how Cheryl Thomas felt about having to withdraw. But how did the rest of the nine candidates featured in "Nine Days of Scandal" fare?

- Alex Johnstone was the first candidate profiled in the "Nine Days of Scandal." She was running for the NDP in Hamilton West–Ancaster–Dundas. She wasn't expected to win but was a strong candidate, hoping to finish second. *TNT* reposted a comment she'd made about a photo of a concrete fence post at Auschwitz. "Ahhh, the infamous Polish, phallic, hydro posts... of course you took pictures of this! It expresses how the curve is normal, natural, and healthy right!" She was called out for making a penis joke about Auschwitz. She wasn't dropped from the ballot, but the NDP vote dropped from 28 percent to 16 percent. She finished third.

- Stefan Jonasson, an NDP candidate in Charleswood–St. James–Assiniboia–Headingley, wasn't so lucky. The NDP dropped him after he made a statement comparing a sect of orthodox Jews to the Taliban. "Much like the Taliban and other extremists, the Haredim offer a toxic caricature of faith, at odds with the spirit of the religious tradition they profess to represent," he posted on Facebook. After agreeing to step down, Jonasson told the CBC, "I wish my party would have stood with me. I think I'm done with politics." The NDP had traditionally done quite well in the Winnipeg-area riding, but after the scandal, a former candidate who replaced Jonasson lost 14 percent of its vote compared to the NDP vote in 2011, ending up with just 6 percent of the vote.

- Conservative candidate Martin Barker was a contender in the riding of Cowichan–Malahat–Langford. *TNT* revealed he had called the province of Quebec a "money pit" and said Bill C-51 (the controversial anti-terrorism act that allowed increased information-sharing between government departments and allowed police to preventatively arrest more people without a warrant) would have prevented the Air India tragedy. Baker was on the ballot, but the Conservatives lost 20 percent of their vote. Barker received 23 percent compared to 43 percent for the Conservatives in 2011. He came third, trailing the NDP winner and the second-place Liberal.

- Liberal Peter Schiefke's "scandal" did him no damage. In response to a woman's post about cleaning her kitchen, he said, "hahahaha........I'm sure you cleaned it up nicely, with you being a women [*sic*] and all!!! It's in your DNA... lol." He was elected in the Quebec riding of Vaudreuil-Soulanges, increasing the Liberal vote by 24 percent over the 2011 results.

- Liberal Kimberley Love—who compared the Alberta oil sands to Mordor from *Lord of the Rings* and posted, under an image from the musical *Springtime for Hitler*

"Springtime for Harper and Canada? Mel Brooks, we've got your next big success right here"—didn't win. Still, she came second and increased her vote share by 22 percent in her Owen Sound riding.

- *TNT* pointed out that Conservative Benjamin Dichter, who ran in Toronto–Danforth, shared a post from a Facebook group called "Crusade Against Islamization of the World," which included the text (not Dichter's words) "Moslems and scums destroying everything in a [*sic*] area in Paris France." The Liberals won the riding in a close race with the NDP. This had been Jack Layton's riding. Benjamin Dichter came third, but he had never been a contender in this riding, anyway.

- Much the same could be said for NDP candidate Nathan Rabidoux, who was running in Perth–Wellington. He made several posts, highlighted by *TNT*, that certainly contrasted with NDP policy. For example: "The next person to talk to me about global warming is getting 50 punches to the head." He also posted, "The Canadian Forces use the C7 Rifle which is basically the M16 with bigger testicles. That's probably the magnificent instrument of democracy you set your hands on at the recruiting booth." The NDP vote dropped 6 percent compared to 2011. Nathan came third with 15 percent of the vote.

- Finally, Peter Njenga was the Liberal candidate in Abbotsford. He posted, "Although my friends consider me to be strong hearted, there are 3 things that I feared (2 being conquered and one yet to be addressed). These fears are: Fear of being loved, fear of height, and fear of water. My wife Jennifer Kube pointed to me that I was not alone in these specific fears because many well-known 'short guys' like me such [sic] Napoleon, Hitler, and Mickey Rooney (the entertainer) were all fearful of love, height and water at one point in time and were helped by women to overcome." He also posted: "How unfair is it that you have worked and build [sic] this nation for over 40 years and then the government decides to give you an Old Age Security Pension and a Guaranteed Income that total $1012 per month, while a refugee receives about $2470 per month. I am not against refugees because we must help those in need, but our citizens come first." He finished second in the Conservative riding, increasing the Liberal vote by 24 percent. Did the *TNT* profile increase his vote share, or was he just riding the Liberal surge?

It's September 2015 and the legendary Harvard campus is showing its fall colours. Daniel Etcovitch is exhausted as he runs down the stairway in Wasserstein Hall between classes. The building is right out of a movie, combining modern and heritage architecture— steel and glass on the stairs, honeyed wood panelling, and heavy doors that date back to another century. His phone rings, and he checks the screen. It's the *Huffington Post.*

He knows what they want. They want to talk about *TNT*'s "Nine Days of Scandal." He feels like he's on a roller coaster; between classes, he's doing two hours of media interviews a day with news outlets across Canada. Journalists in different towns and cities want to talk about their candidates. Within two days, the national media starts to notice. This is north of the border, so Etcovitch is sure no one at Harvard will notice, until one of his professors approaches him after class and asks, "Are you alright?" The professor is from Montréal and is following the Canadian election. He's seen his student on the evening news.

Etcovitch is *TNT*'s chief marketing officer. He's smart, with a big smile, a round face, glasses—like Seth Rogen without the beard—and loves to talk politics. He volunteered on the campaign to elect Liberal MP and former astronaut Marc Garneau.

He remembers the lead-up to their coverage this way. They were in Le Plateau in Montréal, huddled together, watching the newswires and monitoring tips. The election call came on August 4; September 28 was the deadline for candidates to have their names on the ballot.

Etcovitch didn't think the site's "scandal" coverage would lead any candidates to drop out of the race. "We hoped it would have a big impact, but we did not anticipate the partys' reactions. That's not something we saw coming. There were many brand new candidates, and they didn't seem to be very well vetted by the parties or the media. We hoped it would grab eyes."

Even before *True North Times* started doing deep dives into the social media footprints of candidates, other media outlets had begun doing similar investigations. The best Canadian example was "peegate." The CBC-TV consumer affairs show *Marketplace* had aired an episode in 2012 about what service technicians do in people's homes when they are not there. It included footage of a service technician peeing in a cup in someone's kitchen while on the job. He then rinsed out the cup and left it in the sink. Three years later, in September 2015, CBC News received a tip that the service technician in the footage was Conservative candidate Jerry

Bance. CBC News ran the story, and social media blew up with memes, comments, and the hashtag #peegate. The Conservatives very quickly announced Bance was no longer a candidate—all just a few days before "Nine Days of Scandal" was launched.

Robert Jago, a blogger from Montréal, was also using his spare time to dig into the social media history of candidates in 2015. He concentrated his energy on Conservative candidates and dug up a lot of dirt. He revealed that Toronto–Danforth hopeful Tim Dutaud had posted YouTube videos of himself making crank phone calls in which he made fun of people with mental disabilities and pretended to have an orgasm while on the phone with a female customer service representative. Then Jago published his findings about Blair Dale, who was running in Newfoundland. Dale had made controversial comments on social media about race and about women, saying abortion should be limited to women who are sexually assaulted. They were both dropped as candidates by the Conservative Party.

"We were not alone in what we were doing," Etcovitch said, "and we were certainly not the first."

It's hard to know what changed in the fall of 2015. Donald Trump and "fake news" were not yet on the radar. Political parties had been doing "oppo research" as long as citizens had been voting. Political parties were and are always on the lookout for scandals related to sex, money, or serious crimes. Hiding one's criminal past, being caught taking money under the table, or having an affair could get a candidate kicked off the ballot.

Etcovitch says *TNT* received many tips about candidates. They were approached by political parties that wanted to offer them "dirt" on opposition candidates. (They declined; they wanted everything they published to be publicly available.) Also, since they were trying to make politics "fun," they concentrated primarily on new candidates and quirky or absurd opinions or actions.

What about the ethics of what they were doing? Was the goal of getting more youth engaged worth it? Would there be a price, and did they take that into account? Etcovitch says the crew working on "Nine Days" did struggle with that.

"This was a complicated ethical issue for us. The most important thing was that the electorate would have this information." The *TNT* team may have been naive, but they didn't think there would be long-term consequences. "The way we saw it, the consequence would be that it might cause someone to lose some votes or the election."

He says they also felt the information they were revealing was important. "The personal behaviour of these candidates matters because they will represent us. Ultimately, it was more about how candidates and parties reacted rather than what we published."

While all this was happening, I'm ashamed to say my biggest concern was not about what it would mean for the future of democracy or for the media, but what it would mean for my own chances of winning the riding. The first thing I thought when I heard about the Liberals dropping Cheryl Thomas was, "This is good news for me; if I get all those Liberal votes, I might win!"

This, it turns out, was naive on my part.

The Liberal organizers were not so naive. Although she was out of the race, Thomas's name remained on the ballot, and people would vote for her, even though the Liberal Party had made it clear they would not have her in their caucus if she won. It never occurred to me that Liberals would vote for a lame-duck candidate. However, the backroom Liberal organizers in Victoria still wanted to get 10 percent of the vote in order to get back some of the money spent on the campaign. Under Elections Canada's political financing rules, every candidate who receives more than 10 percent of the vote is eligible for a 60 percent rebate on all eligible campaign spending.

If her name hadn't remained on the ballot, I might have picked up those votes. It didn't even enter my mind that the Liberal base would vote Liberal—even when their candidate was not actually in the race. I still wasn't thinking like an experienced politician.

My team was trying to figure out the best way to capture those Liberal votes, but I couldn't shake the feeling that what was happening to Thomas was unfair. I am a journalist. I have a Bachelor of Arts in Political Science and English from Mount Allison University in New Brunswick and a Bachelor of Journalism from Carleton University in Ottawa. During my forty years as a journalist, I have covered politics extensively. The journalist in me wondered, "Whatever she has done, isn't it for the voters to decide? Shouldn't she have a chance to explain?" I called her; she wasn't answering her phone, so I left a message saying I was sorry about what was happening to her. (A few years later she told me she'd heard my message and appreciated the call.)

There's no question her Facebook posts were unacceptable. They were made between 2012 and 2014, when she was living in the Middle East, and were part of a conversation with colleagues about the situation she saw around her. Looking back on it, Thomas later admitted she was naive about how public her posts were. "At the time," she says, "I considered my comments a private conversation with friends. ...I never once felt I needed to clarify that what I was saying was not my official position."

One particular post that was highlighted in reports by *Huffington Post*, CBC, and Global News was the cartoon she shared in 2012 that showed a Black Santa Claus coming down a chimney with the punchline, "You can't have a brown guy with a beard sneaking into your house in the middle of the night! You'd be calling the bomb squad!" What no one reported on at the time is that the thread originated with Canadian comedian Russell Peters, who delivered that punchline during his own Christmas television special.

So what led to the Liberal decision to pull Thomas from the race? Why didn't they allow her to defend herself? In retrospect, she wishes she had defended herself. "This is not about politicians or potential politicians making sure they scrub clean their online presence; it's about what happens when all future politicians are afraid to state their opinions and defend them as part of critical political conversations," she said.

For a political party in the middle of an election, though, the concern is not the future of democracy; the concern is what it will take to win. Party strategists told Thomas they didn't want anything to "distract" from the growing Liberal momentum. This was amplified by the fact that Liberal leader Justin Trudeau was visiting BC and didn't want to have to answer questions on the controversy.

The Liberals could see they were not going to win the riding, but they still had a chance to get the rebate, and they could put volunteers to work in the neighbouring riding of Esquimalt–Saanich–Sooke (ESS), where they had a much better chance of winning. In the end, the Liberals came second in the ESS riding, with 27 percent of the vote; the NDP won, earning 35 percent; from a strategic point of view it had been the right decision to pull Thomas.

We will never know exactly how the *TNT* post changed the outcome in Thomas's Victoria riding, but we do know it made a difference. For example, more than eighteen debates were held over the eleven-week campaign. Those held during the first nine weeks were dynamic—because there were three candidates—me, Thomas, and Rankin—although sometimes it felt like we were shadowboxing, because the Conservative candidate was never present. The debates during the final two weeks were just between Rankin and me, and most of those who attended had already made up their minds. For the undecided, though, it was a dead heat. Rankin and I were good debaters; we knew our platforms and our differences.

Unfortunately, the election was no longer about issues; it was about party loyalty and who could get their supporters to the polls. I'm sure Rankin knew; he was an experienced campaigner. I wasn't. I was still convinced I could dazzle voters with my debating skills, and that voting was about issues and character, not just strategy.

Back at my campaign headquarters, the office is buzzing with the news of "the scandal." The sign on the wall says there are nineteen days left. I pull open the door at 843 Fort Street—the door that has a life-sized picture of me on it. The vast plate glass front window reads "Elect Jo-Ann Roberts" in six-foot letters.

"What do we do now?" I wonder. I see my campaign managers, Sonia Theroux and Stefan Jonsson (not to be confused with Stefan Jonasson, the NDP candidate in Winnipeg from "Nine Days of Scandal"), through the glass walls of their office at the back of the room. They peer at Stefan's computer on his fancy standing desk. I say hi to a couple of volunteers, compliment the new designs of the button-makers who are hard at work, and grab a coffee.

Stefan, Sonia, and I agree to go upstairs to a boardroom; it's less visible, and away from the volunteers and anyone who might drop in. I'm still pumped; they're more serious. They suggest I call a prominent Liberal who's a friend of mine to see if they will take down the Cheryl Thomas sign on their lawn and put up one of mine—and if they will speak to their friends on my behalf.

I make the call. My friend tells me they will take down their Liberal sign but can't put up a Green sign. It's about party loyalty, they say. I'm crushed, although I know they are lifelong Liberals; it is part of their public identity.

I ask my Liberal friend if I can come over for a visit. I'm secretly hoping I can get them to deliver those Liberal votes. We sit on their front patio, hidden from the street by a high hedge and a lovely garden, and I begin to learn what I haven't yet understood about partisan politics. They agree to speak to some of their friends who may be undecided now that the Liberal is not in the race and encourage them to vote for me. They say I would be an excellent MP, but add: "It's too bad you're not running for the Liberals."

I will hear that line a lot over the next six years. Party loyalty is not new, but voters seem to equate political parties with their leaders; if they like a leader, they'll vote for the party, no matter what they think of the individual running in their riding.

Back at the campaign office, the evening door-knocking canvass is getting ready. Maps, walk sheets, brochures, pins, and pens are all packed into green and black bags. I join the team. Knocking on doors is the best way to win votes, but it's hard. I both love it and hate it. It's like being in high school and asking a person you like to go on a date, but you don't ask just one person; you ask person after person. Sometimes the person at the door says no, and sometimes they couldn't care less. It's exhausting. Every once in a while, they say yes. The bonus is when they add, "...and I'll take a sign."

Tonight, I'm paired up with my friend Stefan, who is my co-campaign manager. He was the first person to approach me about the possibility of running for office. It's a lovely evening and everything is going smoothly until we approach a low-rise apartment complex and an older woman in a blue sweater and black pants comes out of a ground-floor unit.

"I want to talk to you," she says forcefully.

I stop and say hello, but she instantly raises her voice and almost spits her words at me. "How dare you decide to run in this riding?" I've heard versions of this accusation a few times this week, so I respond with, "You don't have to vote for me; that's the beauty of democracy."

"I want to vote for you," she says, working herself into a frenzy, "but I also want to vote for Murray Rankin. I don't want to make a choice, and if I don't vote for Murray, the Conservatives might win, and I don't want that!"

Jo-Ann Roberts's "family cheering squad" in Victoria, BC, in October 2015. Clockwise from back R: Christopher Kelly, Meghan Kelly (holding her dog, Moses), Lauren Bercovitch Kelly (holding baby Georgia), Claire Kelly, and Alyson Kelly. [KEN KELLY]

Stefan steps in and assures the woman that, whatever she does with her vote, the Conservatives won't win in Victoria. I thank her for her passion for democracy, and we move on to the next door.

That exchange has stayed with me, and I have thought about it often on other doorsteps and in different elections. That woman was afraid. She didn't want a Conservative MP elected in her riding. In 2015, Stephen Harper was threatening to shut down the CBC; his government was silencing scientists and promising to expand the oil sands. She was afraid of another Conservative majority government.

———

During the campaign's final two weeks, fear repeatedly reared its ugly head in Victoria—to some degree because the Liberals were no longer in the race. Up to that point, it had been a three-way race. As the incumbent, Rankin's job was to convince uncommitted voters to vote for him. That meant emphasizing what an NDP MP would mean for the riding and highlighting his track record. The Liberals were gaining momentum nationally, and Thomas's numbers, according to internal party polling, had been growing. However, when Thomas was no longer a possible winner, the NDP narrative and the party's approach changed.

Now they only had one opponent: me.

I started running into it when I was door-knocking. I guess I should have been flattered that the NDP wasn't telling people I wouldn't be good at the job. Instead, they took the approach that the NDP was the only party that could stop the Conservatives from getting back in power. The overriding message of this campaign for all opposition parties was that Stephen Harper had to go. If a

The Trap of Strategic Voting

A Jo-Ann Roberts campaign sign-waving event with Elizabeth May at the corner of Blanshard and Johnson Streets, Victoria, BC, October 2015. [KEN KELLY]

October 19, 2015. I stand at the corner of Blanshard and Johnson Streets in Victoria with Green Party leader Elizabeth May, who is the MP for the riding next to Victoria, and about twenty supporters. We're waving signs encouraging people to get out and vote. Drivers are waving back and honking their horns. It's 4:30 P.M. on election day.

Hanging out with May is like being with a rock star. People are coming forward to wish her well and to thank her for everything she has done for the planet. A woman approaches; she is in her mid-thirties, slim, has shoulder-length brown hair, and is dressed for the office. She knows May and thanks her for inspiring her, expresses her concern for climate change, and says she wishes she lived in May's riding so she could have voted for her. May turns to her with a touch of alarm in her voice and says, "Well, I hope you voted for Jo-Ann. I need her in Ottawa with me."

The woman's expression turns to grief and her eyes well up with tears when she says, "No, I didn't vote for Jo-Ann. I wanted to, but I had to vote for the NDP because I don't want the Conservatives to win."

May isn't smiling; her lips are drawn in a tight line. The woman says, "I'm sorry; what can I do now?"

May says, "You can go find someone you know who hasn't voted yet and convince them to vote Green."

At that moment, I know in my heart I won't win this election. I also see the regret and despair of a well-informed voter who hasn't voted for what she believes in or for the person she thinks is the best candidate to represent her; she's voted for the candidate she thinks is most likely to defeat the party she doesn't want to form a government.

This moment becomes one of the reasons I will write this book.

Liberal had still been actively running in the riding, she would have been a competitive candidate with a chance of winning.

But with only one real opponent, the NDP saw an opportunity. Their messaging became "vote NDP to stop Harper." Green-leaning voters told me they would vote for me "next time." In hindsight, we should have shifted our campaign message to stress that the Liberals were likely to form a government, so stopping Harper was no longer the issue. Emphasizing the value of a Green MP over an NDP MP would have gone a long way to stopping so-called strategic voting based on fear.

I will never know whether I could have won the Victoria riding had I been more experienced. Rankin was a strong MP, and the riding has a loyal NDP base. But this election gave me valuable and disturbing insight into one of the factors eating away at our democracy—so-called "strategic voting."

In hindsight, we know that dropping Cheryl Thomas didn't hurt the Liberal Party. Justin Trudeau made history; the Liberals went from 36 seats—the fewest seats ever held by a federal party that went on to win the election—to 184 seats and a majority government. This phenomenal surge was in the works when this all happened on the ground in Victoria.

Thomas would receive 8,489 votes: 12 percent of the vote. The Liberal Party in Victoria qualified for the 60 percent rebate of the $36,000 it had spent before Thomas was dropped. The Victoria Liberal Electoral District Association (EDA) received a rebate of $21,000, which it could use to prepare for the next election.

But the loss of the Liberal candidate definitely did affect how the election in that riding unfolded. "Nine Days of Scandal" had an impact on the political landscape in Canada. And although it raised some important questions, that type of scandalmongering is a symptom of an ailing democracy.

How can we make Canada's democracy healthy again? Perhaps a good place to start is with the growing influence of pre-election polling.

CHAPTER 2

MARGIN OF ERROR

Polling and Prognosticating

M ARKING A SIMPLE *X* ON A BALLOT CAN CHANGE THE fate of a person, a nation—even the state of the world.

Grabbing a tiny golf pencil and placing a mark beside the name of a person who might run the city or the province or the country is a superpower many of us take for granted—and which some of us have sadly given up altogether. In Canada's 2021 federal election, more than 11 million eligible people didn't vote. Almost one-third of eligible voters shrugged their shoulders and said, "Whatever other people decide is okay with me." I find that mind-blowing. Others, like the woman I spoke with at the corner of Blanshard and Johnson who voted strategically in 2015, treat voting as if they are picking their Lotto 649 numbers—calculating who will win and voting accordingly.

There was a time when deciding how to vote was as simple as knowing one's family's preference for the Liberals or the

Conservatives. There is a reason we sometimes refer to "safe" seats in Canada. Political affiliation was inherited from your parents and their parents before them.

That tradition has largely disappeared; most people now feel free to vote with their conscience. So what influenced the remorseful voter in Victoria in 2015? Why did she feel that, instead of voting for the candidate she preferred, she had to vote NDP to prevent the Conservatives from forming the government?

The simple answer is that polling, and the way the campaigns and the media used those polls, influenced her vote.

Late in the 2015 election, the national polls were showing a tight race. From October 6 through 9, the Liberals and Conservatives were tied if the margin of error was taken into account. By the campaign's final week, the Liberals had taken a statistical lead. These polls were reported by the Canadian Press in the October 16, 2015, *Victoria Times Colonist*:

> *Since Oct. 9, six different polling firms have placed the Liberals at the top of the leaderboard with public support in the mid-30s, while Conservative party support held steady around 30 per cent and the New Democrats polled in the mid- to low 20s. Only pollsters Angus Reid Institute and Forum Research have showed Conservative leads in the last week and both had the Liberals and Tories bunched within the margin of error.*

The polls were being used by the political parties to influence the vote—even for my own campaign. The Green Party ran afoul of Elections Canada rules on the day before the vote in 2015 when it produced twelve hundred flyers in my riding of Victoria which read: "It's a two-way race—the choice is yours, Victoria," and went on to say that, based on the latest polling results, NDP candidate Murray Rankin (the New Democrat) was ahead of me by a single percentage point.

That poll was taken on October 13, 2015. What the flyer failed to mention was how the poll was conducted and that it had a margin of error of ± 9.8 percent—a very high margin.

What determines the margin of error? Essentially, it's determined by sample size—the larger the sample, the lower the margin—but some other factors, such as "weighting," come into play. Polls tend to overrepresent people who are easier to get in touch with, which is not truly representative of the general population. Weighting is a mathematical way of balancing the numbers and is critical to obtaining less-biased results, but it also increases the margin of error.

Leaving out the critical information about the margin of error is a violation of Elections Canada rules. The poll was intended for internal party use, but in the heat of the final days of the election, the Green Party national campaign office decided to put it out. In haste, the qualifiers were left out.

I didn't see the flyer, but the NDP did—and reported it to Elections Canada. Even though I hadn't approved it, everything done in my name is my responsibility. On the day of the election, I was told what had happened, and the party took full responsibility for the erroneous flyer. In compliance with an order from Elections Canada, the party released a public statement apologizing and acknowledging the breach and explaining that "the flyer was intended as an invitation for Conservative supporters to vote strategically for the Green Party candidate." It's ironic that the Green Party—itself so affected by strategic voting and polling—found itself using both to try to win the seat. Such is the nature of the first-past-the-post system. Ultimately, the poll was correct; I lost, not by 1 percent, but by 10 percent, which was within the margin of error. The NDP won all of the seats on the Island except Saanich Gulf Island, which was won by Green Party leader Elizabeth May.

Four years later, on October 16, 2019, another poll would bring me to tears—and I can assure you it takes a lot to make me cry during a campaign.

It's Wednesday. I'm in bed, waiting for my husband to deliver my first cup of coffee. (Yes, I'm spoiled, but he knows the way to my heart.) I'm scrolling through my Facebook feed when I see it. Suddenly, there's a post that puts a dagger through my heart.

A loyal supporter, who has a big "Jo-Ann Roberts" sign on his lawn, and who has donated $1,000 to my campaign, is announcing to his nine hundred followers that he will vote *strategically*.

I feel like I am going to throw up. Not again! This isn't some faceless person who is undecided, or a voter I have never met. This is a supporter—a business owner with a wide circle of friends. He likes me.

His post reads:

> *There are times when strategic voting makes sense. We have a broken electoral system. The Liberals promised they*

*would work to fix it. They did not.... I have supported Jo-Ann
Roberts through the election, and I am optimistic for a great
forward motion for the Green Party of Canada. But, now in
HALIFAX, if this best available information is near accurate,
we have a real chance of making a difference and changing
the shape of things to come in a dramatic way. I will now be
voting NDP for that reason.*

I am devastated. All I can do is cry. I have no idea how to fight
this, and there is so little time left: the election is in five days. But
I know I have to get up and do something, so I dry my eyes on my
husband's handkerchief, drink my coffee, and decide my pity party
is over.

I hit the phones. I call the campaign team and ask them to meet
me in the office in an hour. I also send a note to the man I feel has
devastated my chances by announcing he is voting for the NDP,
and I beg him to call me ASAP.

Following the Facebook trail, we discover that my friend's decision had been influenced by a concerted NDP campaign using
data from *338Canada*, a website that uses a complex algorithm
to publish electoral projections based on opinion polls, electoral
history, and demographic data. An NDP supporter had publicly
posted on Facebook and sent it to several "friends voting in Halifax,
Dartmouth/Cole Harbour," suggesting that they should consider
voting strategically because "the Greens aren't close to winning,
but the combined Green and NDP vote would easily win the seat."

The information didn't come from a poll. There hadn't been any
public polls done in Halifax. I'm sure the big parties had internal
polls, but no local polls were available. The post was a graph pro-
jecting the popular vote in Halifax. It showed the Liberals at 35.4
percent with a margin of error of 7.3 percent and the NDP at 35.2

percent with a margin of error of 7.7 percent. The GPC—that's me—was at 14.1 percent with a margin of error of 4.7 percent, and the Conservatives at 13.1 percent, with a margin of error of 4.1 percent.

I should have been thrilled. Greens in Halifax traditionally polled at around 4 percent. Being in third place and in the double digits was a considerable improvement. But all I could see was the Liberal–NDP tie. With a margin of error of almost 8 percent, they might have been much farther apart, but I knew that wasn't how the public would see it. This graph would be reported as a tight race, and the strategic voting would begin. I knew that, just as my former "supporter" had done, a lot of voters would decide to try to break the tie.

It's essential at this point to understand how political candidates like me think. Every vote matters, and I still wanted to do as well as I could—even if I wasn't going to win.

One thing about elections is that they're not over until the polls close, no matter what your heart says. In the office, I ask the team what we should do. Should we commission our own poll? In truth, there was no more money in the bank, and a poll would cost $5,000. The wise advice from those who had been in the backrooms of other parties and had seen plenty of elections was that it was too late. If we were going to do it, we should have done it the previous week.

It was agreed that I should talk to the person who had made the public post. I knew my supporter had been swayed by the *338Canada* information because he had made his decision public, but I had no idea how many people were considering doing the same thing. I couldn't call every voter who may have seen the graph, or anyone who now planned to vote strategically. I did my best to

Jo-Ann Roberts at a Halifax, NS, polling station, voting in the federal election on October 21, 2019. [KEN KELLY]

address it when I could with social media and door-knocking, but it was a silent vote-killer. It infected voters like a virus.

For the record, the results in Halifax in 2019 were pretty close to what *338Canada* had projected, if the margin of error is taken into account. The Liberals won with 42 percent of the vote, the NDP came second with 30 percent, and I came third with 14.3 percent. Even without a poll, the *338Canada* algorithm that had projected the vote was very accurate, but the way it had been used and interpreted was all over the map. I wanted to find out more about how *338Canada* worked.

Philippe Fournier loves to talk about this stuff. Fournier, with his made-for-TV good looks—dark-rimmed glasses, curly white hair, and five o'clock shadow at ten in the morning—teaches physics and astrophysics at Cégep de Saint-Laurent, a post-secondary institution in Montréal. He has a slight French accent and apologizes for his English, which is excellent.

Fournier remembers in detail the events that led him to create *338Canada* and its French-language equivalent, *Qc125*. During an interview, he told me it was during the 2016 Trump–Clinton election.

"I was following the election every day; it was very addictive," he told me. "I am an astrophysicist and my lab work during my studies was to crunch numbers and write computer programs to analyze images from the sky, and so I started doing a little programming myself. I had an Excel spreadsheet. It was very rudimentary at first, following the daily polls during the Trump–Clinton election, and I was pulling my hair out, looking at, not the polls, but the coverage of the polls. It was clear that Mrs. Clinton was the favourite, but she was not an overwhelming favourite, as outlets were presenting it to be."

He told his friends and family that it was possible that Trump would win. When Trump did win with a small margin, Fournier said he was floored that "no one saw it coming."

The seed was planted. He saw a need for an algorithm that could combine poll results to get a more accurate analysis.

A few weeks later, Fournier saw an article in a Montréal newspaper about a Quebec poll. It made his blood boil. "It was just so badly written, not knowing what the margins of error were, the uncertainty, the nature of polls. It was probably a new journalist that never did any math or quantitative method that was given an assignment by an editor."

Fournier told his students he was going to do something about it. He felt there was a need for more science in the polling industry and in the media. He started a blog on polling—variations, fluctuations, and uncertainty. The charming astrophysicist became popular in Quebec, and the media started inviting him to be a regular guest for discussions about polling.

Then came the Montréal municipal election in 2017. The polls indicated that the incumbent, former MP and federal cabinet minister Denis Coderre, would easily win a second term over newcomer Valérie Plante. When Fournier dug into the details of the polls, he thought Coderre could be in trouble—that was the headline of his blog post in August. He repeated it a couple of months later when the polls showed Coderre's lead starting to narrow. When Valérie Plante won, it surprised many, but not Fournier. His successful prediction of the Valérie Plante win increased his media exposure. It also convinced Fournier that he could apply his technique to other elections.

Elections were held in Ontario and Quebec in 2018, and he wrote a program aggregating data from the Canadian census. He was trying to find trends that could be codified, and it worked—*Qc125* and *338Canada* were born.

He explains it this way: "I had 90 percent [of] the right winners in the Ontario election, and then the same in Quebec. So, it's not perfect. I like to say to people it's not made to be perfect. It's statistics. If I have a perfect election, it's an outlier." His predictions are now key players in every major election in Canada. Some Canadians see him as the man with a political crystal ball. He is, for many, the populist face of polls.

In an election campaign, the media plays a critical role in calling the race. Having pundits like Fournier on the team offers an advantage because most media outlets can no longer afford to commission individual surveys that would give them the depth they need to provide accurate coverage. Fournier has been a regular contributor to *Maclean's*, *L'actualité*, and *Politico*.

Similarly, Éric Grenier now runs an elections analysis site called *The Writ* (thewrit.ca); he was a polls analyst for CBC from 2014 to 2021 and is still a regular guest on the network. Like Fournier, Grenier takes available polls and analyzes them according to a formula posted on the site. His inspiration came from a similar blog in the US called *FiveThirtyEight.com* (now owned by ABC News), which was started by a statistician and poker player named Nate Silver. Silver was named one of the "100 most influential people" by *Time* magazine in 2009 after an election forecasting system he developed successfully predicted the outcomes in forty-nine of the fifty states in the 2008 US presidential election. In the 2012 US presidential election, his system correctly predicted the winners in all fifty states.

These three people have created a new category in the field of polls and elections—aggregators. The concept is not new; academics and researchers have, since the 1970s, taken polls of polls. But it wasn't until aggregators started working with media outlets that we saw a shift in how polling was perceived and used by voters and special interest groups.

Éric Grenier speculates that the popularity of poll pundits and polling aggregators demonstrates that the public wants to have more information available during an election campaign. The key question is, does this information influence the vote?

I suggested to Fournier that perhaps no polls should be released publicly during the writ period because they have an undue influence on voters. Not surprisingly, Fournier disagrees. He says doing that would be like playing hockey and not announcing the score until the end. He says both the players and the teams need to know the score to help them decide how to react—do they need to play harder or maybe pull the goalie?

Whether or not that argument holds water, his next point does. He says when polls are done correctly, they are just information. He admits they can be manipulated, but adds it's essential that pollsters be held accountable. The best way to do that, he says, is to compare polling results from the last week of the election with the actual results of the election.

"The alternative to having polls is to keep people in the dark," says Fournier. "How about those signs out there on the trees and the highways, the ads that I just heard on the radio or on Facebook? Everything during a campaign is spin...and a poll is the only measurable objective information that is available."

He says when pollsters get it wrong, and they do occasionally, it generally leads to consequences for that pollster. "It's the Darwinism of polling. If you're bad at polling, people won't give you money to poll anymore," he says, noting that the worst polling firms have largely "gone the way of the dodo."

I can't help but think of that cliché used by so many politicians: the only poll that matters is the one on election day. It turns out that's not entirely true, but it is the one that keeps pollsters honest.

Back to October 16, 2019, when the graph on the *338Canada* site has me in tears. Fournier says the only way he could have avoided presenting a graph with such a high margin of error would have been to have access to more local polls. He points out that if a reputable company does a poll with a solid methodology, it will be picked up by a site like his and that will lower the margin of error. The difficulty is that no party wants to release the results of a poll that shows they're behind, and polls cost money. Larger parties with bigger budgets have an advantage, not only because they can afford to commission polls and therefore have more information about how and where to target their campaign efforts, but also because they are better represented in polling at both national and local levels.

⸻

During the week before the federal election in 2019, the *338Canada* site had 10 million views. I was one of those viewers and, believe me, I didn't like what this site was doing to my campaign. (I might have been heard to utter, "A pox on all their polling houses!") Although I felt then that Canada should consider not allowing polls to be made public during the writ period, I no longer hold that opinion. As a journalist and an active politician, I know that information is valuable. Philippe Fournier is right when he says there are all kinds of elements in a campaign that we use to influence voters: signs, flyers, and social media posts. The important thing is that there are rules for these: the costs must be made public; signs must be authorized by an official agent for the candidate, et cetera. (Interestingly, political ads don't fall under the truth in advertising legislation, but many MPs are working to change that.)

Rules do exist around making opinion polls public. These rules, monitored by Elections Canada, say the first person or media outlet to release results *must* include the details of how the poll was done, including who conducted it, when and where it was done, the sample size, and the margin of error, as well as where the public can get a copy of the entire survey. Any print or internet site that publishes the results must include the wording of the questions asked and provide instructions on how readers can obtain the written report. Any media outlet that broadcasts or publishes the poll within twenty-four hours of its initial publication must do the same. Poll results cannot be published on election day.

Most voters don't check the fine print or the web links, which is where those details generally end up. Their eyes glaze over when they hear the margin of error is ± 3 percent, nineteen times out of twenty. Headlines like "Liberals Pull Ahead of Conservatives" dominate, and little attention is paid to the margin of error.

So, what is the best way to ensure that the public understands what they are seeing and that the pollsters and aggregators provide information that is as accurate as possible? To improve the quality of the information, aggregators have begun to rank the performance of competing polling companies. Philippe Fournier says companies were unhappy when he gave them less than an A rating, but it led them to improve their standards to ensure their best work was available to him and other aggregators.

The Canadian Research Insights Council (CRIC) has established guidelines for the polling industry. Dozens of polling companies are listed as members; the organization also provides guidelines to assist journalists in assessing polling information. However, there is no legislation that allows this organization to impose sanctions other than withdrawing membership from a polling company that doesn't meet the CRIC standards.

VOTING REVOLUTION TIP

When considering polling results, ask yourself: Do these results disclose the details of how the poll was done, who conducted it, when and where it was done, the sample size, and the margin of error, and do they say where I can get a copy of the entire survey?

How do we safeguard fair elections and make sure the public gets the right information when it comes to polling in Canada? I think the answer lies in looking at what polling companies tend to get wrong, or at least what the public finds confusing.

Philippe Fournier points to one election where he did get it wrong—and where he wishes he'd withdrawn the data when it became evident there was not enough information to make qualified predictions. The Nova Scotia general election of August 2021 was the first miss for the *338Canada* algorithm. Only thirty-five of fifty-five winners were called correctly; four others were within the margin of error. The *338Canada* site predicted a Liberal minority or majority; in the end, the PCs won a slim majority, with thirty-one seats (twenty-eight are required for a majority). The *338Canada* model had too little information to go on, which led to a very high margin of error.

So here's my practical advice: I suggest that Elections Canada revise its regulations related to poll reporting. Rather than simply reporting the margin of error, the rules should not allow media outlets and social media to publish poll results when the margin of error exceeds a particular number. A margin of error of more than, say, ± 5 indicates that a pollster is in uncertain territory, and an effort should be made to increase the certainty before the poll can be published.

VOTING REVOLUTION TIP

Encourage Elections Canada to limit the margin of error of polls that can be released during a campaign period and revise its regulations so media outlets cannot publish poll results when the margin of error exceeds a particular number (such as ± 5).

Also, while it is encouraging to see the CRIC establish standards for the industry, there is no legal obligation for polling or market research companies to be members, and therefore no way for the public to assess the quality of the work being done by these practitioners. The work of the highest-profile and best-known companies is very public; companies like Nanos, Mainstreet, Angus Reid, Leger, and Ipsos are recognized and trusted by both the media and the public. But there are other companies doing this work that are not. We may have reached a time in our political maturity as a country where a company that wants to take the pulse of the electorate not only has to register with CRTC to make calls but also must have some form of professional designation that is mandatory and managed by an independent body or an industry organization that reports to a federal oversight department.

David Zussman, adjunct professor at the School of Public Administration, University of Victoria, and senior fellow at the Graduate School of Public and International Affairs, University of Ottawa, told the CRIC that "election polls are part of a feedback loop voters expect at election time to understand the dynamics of the campaign. They play an important role in modern democracies."

He added, "The more quality polling we have in Canada, the better."

I agree, but the key word there is "quality," and we must do better.

~~~~~

To finish my tale of the day of the disastrous poll, I did get in touch with my supporter—the one with my sign on his lawn—and we discussed his decision to vote strategically. In the end, he changed his mind and voted Green—and went so far as to post on his Facebook page that he was doing so. The day after the election, he wrote, "Jo-Ann Roberts and the presence of all Green party candidates definitely made a difference—is making a difference. In a country where over 66 percent voted for another party than the one that will form the government, the process and the math of voting will, eventually, have to change. I think Jo-Ann would have been the best person we could have sent to Ottawa."

It made me feel better and convinced me we can do better. If voters who are engaged feel the pressure to vote strategically rather than for the person they want to represent them, it's not a big leap to understand why people who feel the outcome is already decided don't make the effort to vote at all—because they don't believe it will make a difference.

Teamwork at its best: Jo-Ann Roberts with her husband, Ken Kelly, at the Fridays for Future Climate March in Halifax, NS, on September 27, 2019. Thousands of people turned out for the rally. [AUTHOR COLLECTION]

CHAPTER 3

A PILLAR OF DEMOCRACY

The Critical Role of a Free Press

Because of the constant bombardment of media of all forms every moment of every day it is impossible for us to ignore it and subconsciously it is slowly becoming our master.

– Prescient grade 7 student Jo-Ann Roberts
(still working on her grammar and punctuation), April 1969

I WAS TWELVE YEARS OLD WHEN I WROTE THOSE WORDS— pretty serious stuff for a kid who wasn't yet a teenager. I was a junior high school student at Prince Charles School in the working-class city of Saint John, NB. It was my third school in three years, but I was used to being the new kid in school. As a United Church minister, my dad's assignments kept changing. During my first week at Prince Charles, a kid from my class punched the on-duty teacher during recess on the asphalt square we called a playground.

It was going to be an interesting year.

Since I was new, I had no friends and lots of time to think about serious subjects. So when my English teacher, Mr. Hughes, announced that there would be a public speaking contest, I signed up. I had done some public speaking at my last school, and it sounded fun. There wasn't much interest at Prince Charles, so maybe it wasn't surprising that Mr. Hughes encouraged me to enter.

The contest included students from across the province. There was a list of four topics to choose from. I chose "Mass media today—man's servant or master?" over "My concept of an ideal vacation" or "The most interesting section of the library."

I won our school contest. I was excited, but that didn't last long. On my way out of the room where the contest had been held, one of the teachers, Mr. D., who had been a judge, approached me.

"You shouldn't have won," he said. "You were terrible at the impromptu speech. They'll eat you up at Districts."

Tough school. Survival of the fittest. It was a foretaste of my future as a journalist and a politician.

Over the next week, I practised impromptu speeches every night after supper. My parents would do the dishes and throw out topics for me to talk about for precisely one minute. The practice paid off; I won the district competition. (Take that, Mr. D.!) But I faced a challenge as I headed into the provincial finals in the junior division. As it turned out, I was the youngest in the competition and the only student to pick a serious topic. Despite that, or maybe because of it, the judges gave me high marks for my prepared and impromptu speeches.

I concluded in my presentation that "mass media today is strictly man's master." I also warned that television was the greatest form of mass media. "It is estimated that a child in their school years will watch fifteen thousand hours of television, and during that time, he will read only ten novels." And I pointed out, "A man no longer buys a product for its quality, but for the image of it advertising has created in his mind." (The lack of inclusive language in my speech is quite jarring today.)

I won again. The next day, a picture of me with my trophy was published in the newspaper. Very satisfying!

My interest in politics also started when I was quite young. The year before we moved to Saint John, we lived in Charlottetown, PEI. I was in grade 6, and I wrote a story for my English teacher in the form of a news report from twenty years in the future. It reported, "The voting computers had just tallied up the final ballots.... The delegates attending the Liberal leadership convention had just elected Miss Jo-Ann Roberts, age thirty-one, as Canada's first female Prime Minister." The story concluded, "In her acceptance speech, the new Prime Minister thanked the delegates for their support and pledged to them a new dawn in Canadian foreign affairs and the status of women and youth."

I got an A. I guess the teacher didn't want to mess with the future PM! It's interesting that I had a sense there would be computers in 1988 and that, at age eleven, I cared about the status of women—and that I wrote the piece as a newspaper story. While I'm sure I didn't give it much thought then, I seemed to know innately that democracy and journalism were linked.

Luckily, my mother kept the pink, wide-ruled Hilroy scribbler in which I wrote this story in pencil, complete with spelling mistakes. My mom also kept a copy of my speech from the public speaking contest. Unlike the essay in the pink scribbler, this speech was written in ink, in a much neater hand, with a fountain pen. It includes words underlined in red for emphasis, and whole paragraphs are crossed out to keep me within the three-minute time limit. There is also a typewritten copy of the speech in my mom's file. My dad's secretary must have typed it up after my win, because it's labelled,

"Winning Speech in the Junior Division." The pages have yellowed and the staple has rusted, but there is a warning in the words I spoke as a precocious twelve-year-old.

The speech contest had taken place in April 1969, around the time philosopher Marshall McLuhan had suggested "the medium is the message" in his book *Understanding Media: The Extensions of Man.* Print was still alive and well, but there was a concern that television would wipe out radio. McLuhan was looking at how the message would change depending on the platform. We know now he was way ahead of his time.

The contest was also just a few years before the Watergate scandal that made the work of two investigative reporters, Bob Woodward and Carl Bernstein, famous. When I saw the movie about their work, *All the President's Men,* starring Robert Redford and Dustin Hoffman, I was convinced that being a journalist was a way to make a difference in the world.

I was fortunate that in 1969 we had a neighbour who worked for the National Film Board. When I was writing my speech, he agreed to let me interview him as part of my research. He talked about the role of the editor in creating a story and explained how the same images could be arranged differently to tell a different story. He talked about how the opinions and perspectives of the reporter make a difference in selecting the storyline, and emphasized the importance of journalists being held to account.

It was an eye-opening experience in media literacy for a kid who was mostly just a fan of *Laugh-In* and *Bonanza.*

A free press is an essential pillar of a democratic society. This is spelled out in the *Canadian Charter of Rights and Freedoms*. Section two of the Charter outlines the fundamental freedoms that must be protected: "Freedom of conscience, freedom of religion, freedom of thought, freedom of belief, freedom of expression, freedom of the press and of other media of communication, freedom of peaceful assembly, and freedom of association." It also says the rights and freedoms set out in the Charter are "subject only to such reasonable limits prescribed by law as can be demonstrably justified in a free and democratic society."

Maria Ressa is a Filipino and American journalist and author, and the co-founder and CEO of *Rappler*, an online newspaper in the Philippines. She spent nearly two decades as a lead investigative reporter for CNN in Southeast Asia and is a recipient of the Nobel Peace Prize. In her acceptance speech for the Nobel Prize, she talked about the loss of a free press as a threat to democracy. "Without facts, you can't have truth; without truth, you can't have trust. Without trust, we have no shared reality, no democracy," she said. "The greatest need today is to transform that hate and violence—the toxic sludge that's coursing through our information eco-system, prioritized by American internet companies that make more money by spreading that hate and triggering the worst in us."

As truckers converged on Ottawa, honking their horns and disrupting lives in February 2022, Ressa's argument was borne out. The so-called "Freedom Convoy" truckers were engaged and enraged. They felt they weren't being heard, and their frustration needed an outlet. A popular slogan during the protest, painted on the tailgate of a dump truck in three-foot letters, was "the media is the virus." The protesters threatened members of the mainstream media and called them liars. Fox News in the US reported that organizers of the convoy had banned mainstream media outlets from attending the convoy's first press conference; organizers did not invite CBC, CTV, or the *Toronto Star* because they said these outlets reported "fake news."

In fact, those outlets were carrying a story about a GoFundMe site through which the convoy had raised millions of dollars; the funds had been frozen because, as GoFundMe said in a statement, "We now have evidence from law enforcement that the previously peaceful demonstration has become an occupation, with police reports of violence and other unlawful activity." This news was not fake at all. GoFundMe took down the Freedom Convoy page after dispersing $1 million of the $10 million raised. The remaining funds were returned to donors.

Truckers converged on Ottawa in a so-called "Freedom Convoy" in February 2022.
[Maksim Sokolov (Maxergon), CC BY-SA 4.0, via Wikimedia Commons]

Making people angry, giving them someone to blame, and giving them a champion is one way to get people involved in politics—as we have seen in the United States with the rise of Donald Trump. Trump even went so far as to say journalists are the "enemy of the people." We also saw the danger in this kind of approach. Violence is not the answer, but if politicians make citizens mad enough, fan a flame enough—they will storm the Capitol. It was ironic that many of the rioters who stormed the US Capitol building in Washington on January 6, 2021, screaming, "Stop the Steal"—referring to the results of the presidential election—had not voted themselves.

If journalists are doing their jobs well, there will be times when they will upset people; sometimes the truth—in this case, telling protesters that vaccine mandates were effective, vaccines were safe, and masks save lives—hurts. Being criticized and disliked is an occupational hazard for journalists. Public frustration and anger are understandable, but in a healthy democracy no one's life should be threatened for doing their job.

Rita Trichur, a business columnist at the *Globe and Mail*, reported on social media that she had received a threatening message after writing about how COVID-19 vaccine mandates and documentation fraud affected businesses. "The sender inquired if I had children, told me that I was on 'a list' and said that I wouldn't be forgotten," she wrote. "Some people complain about 'cancel culture,' but some of us actually worry about being killed."

In a video interview on Global News, one of the Freedom Convoy supporters told a reporter, "You are the enemy of the people. You are the vile liars," and called for the journalist to be tried and executed along with other journalists.

What is disturbing about these stories is that they reinforce the mantra of the disenfranchised: the mainstream media is not to be trusted. But what if the CBC, the *New York Times*, the *Globe and Mail*, and the *Washington Post* did not exist?

Sarah Repucci was a senior director for research and analysis at Freedom House, a Washington, DC–based organization that works to defend human rights and promote democratic change around the world, with a focus on political rights and civil liberties. She authored a report called *Media Freedom: A Downward Spiral*, and she noted that media freedom has been deteriorating around the world over the past decade, with populist political leaders overseeing attempts to "throttle the independence of the media sector." She concluded, "While the threats to global media freedom are real and concerning in their own right, their impact on the state of democracy is what makes them truly dangerous."

This problem has been growing. In October 2021, the Canadian Association of Journalists (CAJ) and the Canadian Journalism Foundation (CJF) held a round table on journalists and online hate. Close to one hundred journalists from across the country took part. The report on that event was (ironically) released while the Freedom Convoy was attacking journalists in Ottawa. The report that came from that round table called for media companies to offer better protection for their journalists and to establish protocols for dealing with online hate. It also calls on government, law enforcement, and social media platforms to act.

Some may disagree, but I would argue that one of the best ways to protect the freedom of the press is to have a strong, independent public broadcaster. To be transparent, I spent much of my career working with Canada's national public broadcaster, the CBC. I have also worked in print journalism, as a freelance writer, and as a documentary producer, but more than half of my forty years in journalism were at the "Mother Corp."

I remember the day I started as a CBC Radio reporter. It was September 1978, in Saint John, NB—a decade after I wrote my award-winning speech on the media. I was twenty-two years old and nervous as I entered the new CBC offices in Hilyard Place. The station had just opened; most of the staff were new. The studio and reception desks were at the front, followed by the manager's office, then a stretch of space with three groupings of four or five metal desks. I soon learned that these groupings represented the morning show, the noon show, and the newsroom. There was a wall of windows stretching the entire length of the office. I walked toward the back wall where a series of teletype machines clicked away, spewing yellow newsprint that piled up on the floor. About five feet off the floor, above the machines, was a board with about five spikes, one every foot or so. News stories that had been ripped off the machines hung on each of the spikes. I saw two men in their forties, wearing suit jackets and ties, eyeing me as I approached. One had a cigarette dangling from his hand. "Here she comes—the new reporter," he said, then added with an exasperated sigh, "she's green AND she's a woman! Lucky us."

Another tough crowd.

I was a hard worker, and it didn't take long to win them over. I spent the next four years working with these outstanding reporters, John Miller and Mark Pedersen. I grew to love them both. They were kind and generous, and they taught me the very essence of what it means to be a good reporter. Our motto in that newsroom was "get it first, but first, get it right." We typed out our stories on yellow newsprint with two layers of carbon paper to produce three copies of every story. We then had to retype them into the teletype machine to send them to other stations, including the national newsroom in Toronto. I cut audio tape with a razor blade and fixed our edits with sticky tape. Looking back on it now, I am amazed at how much news we could turn out daily.

I left the CBC in 1982 when my first child was born. Those were the days when employees were given just a few weeks of maternity leave, so if I wanted to take a year to raise a child, I had to quit my job. I freelanced for the next decade and had three more children before I went back to the CBC in 1994, hosting CBC Radio's *Information Morning* (serving the eastern half of New Brunswick) out of Moncton. I held the job for ten years and, in 2004, moved to Victoria, BC, to host *All Points West*, the CBC Radio afternoon show for all of British Columbia except Vancouver. In 2014, at age fifty-eight, I took early retirement.

I saw a lot of changes in the CBC over those four decades. In the 1970s and '80s, CBC knew what it was about. It played a vital role in the fabric of the country. Local radio was strong. In 1974, it became ad-free, which changed the service's nature. It was no longer serving commercial interests. It was well-staffed, reasonably well-funded, and clearly understood its place in the media landscape. We were there to tell the stories of Canadians at home and to bring a Canadian perspective to stories abroad. We were rooted in the regions and free to take risks that might cost us ratings—a luxury our colleagues in the private sector did not enjoy.

*On April 25, 2014, the crew at CBC Victoria celebrated Jo-Ann Roberts's twenty years of uninterrupted service at the CBC. Back row, L–R: Bob MacDonald, Khalil Akhtar, Michael Tymchuk, Peter Hutchinson, Gregor Craigie, Jean Paetkau, and Sophie Rousseau. Front row, L– R: Lisa Cordasco, Amanda Heffelfinger, Idil Mussa, Deborah Wilson, Jo-Ann Roberts, Kelly Nakatsuka, Kirstie Hudson, Bea Britneff. [*KEN KELLY*]*

In 2012, I was awarded the Harvey S. Southam journalist-in-residence lectureship at the University of Victoria. The position allowed me to create and teach a course about any important issue in journalism in Canada. I developed a course on the value of public broadcasting to democracy. I was also responsible for giving the Harvey S. Southam Lecture, a public lecture on the same aspect of the topic I was teaching. My public lecture was called "Making the Case for the CBC."

The lecture almost didn't happen. I had been teaching about public broadcasting for a whole semester. I worked three days a week at UVic and two days a week at my CBC Radio job as host of the provincial afternoon show. The day before the lecture, I tweeted on my CBC account to promote the lecture. The tweet was a bit of a tease. "Do you know how CBC funding compares to other public broadcasters worldwide?" it said. "Find out at UVic tomorrow at 7:30 pm. #makingthecaseforCBC." The tweet was a mistake, not because it was incorrect, but because I made it from my CBC Twitter account. My boss, the station manager, called me into his office the next day and asked to see a copy of my speech. I asked why. He said CBC management in Toronto had seen my tweet and worried about what I might say.

I was very upset by this, primarily because I felt the institution where I had worked for decades suddenly didn't seem to trust me. But it's important to note that Stephen Harper was prime minister then, and the Conservative government had been severely cutting the CBC's budget. CBC management didn't want a lone-wolf employee on Vancouver Island causing trouble and tweeting about it.

Of course, that's not how I saw it at the time. I told my boss he couldn't see my speech. I assured him anything I said would be accurate and well-documented, and he would have to trust me on that. After all, they had given me a live mic for three hours a day for eighteen years, and I hadn't embarrassed them yet. The station manager, a great guy, said he'd reassure management that there would be no more tweets and that he'd see me at the speech that night. I'm glad I didn't back down, but I admit I went into the lecture that night with a bit of dread.

The speech went well, and everyone learned what the CBC brass was nervous about. At thirty-three dollars per capita, Canada ranked seventeenth out of twenty Western countries in terms of per-capita public funding for public broadcasters.

This story says something about the influence of government funding on journalism. CBC management was genuinely worried about what would happen if an employee embarrassed the government or if the CBC was seen to be using its government-subsidized resources to lobby for increased support for itself.

And there was reason to worry. While a Conservative government had created the CBC in 1932, the Harper years were particularly difficult for CBC/Radio Canada. Under the Harper government, in 2012, the CBC's federal funding of $1.1 billion was cut by $115 million over three years. Twelve hundred jobs were lost. When Erin O'Toole was elected leader of the Conservative Party of Canada (CPC) in 2020, one of his platform planks was to "defund the CBC." Pierre Poilievre promised to do the same in 2024.

Cuts have also taken place under Liberal governments. Prime Ministers Paul Martin and Jean Chrétien cut CBC funding in the 1990s as part of a deficit-cutting campaign. This meant that a much leaner public broadcaster already existed at the time of the Conservative cuts, so in many ways, they hurt more. The Liberal government under Justin Trudeau restored some funding to the CBC. The CBC's government funding for the 2024–2025 budget was $1.4 billion.

While the budgets change, the mandate of the CBC has stayed the same. The Broadcasting Act states that "the Canadian Broadcasting Corporation, as the national public broadcaster, should provide radio and television services incorporating a wide range of programming that informs, enlightens and entertains." The act also outlines that CBC/Radio-Canada should be predominantly Canadian and serve the unique needs of the country's regions. It must also be of equivalent quality in English and French and meet the needs of linguistic minorities while reflecting Canada's multi-racial and multicultural nature.

It's actually remarkable that Canada's national public broad-caster does all these things equally in two official languages, offers programming in eight Indigenous languages, and broadcasts in five languages on its web-based international radio service, Radio Canada International (RCI). We do it in Canada with less funding than countries that broadcast in one language and, in many cases, a single time zone. The cost to every Canadian is $33 per person per year. The BBC in the UK costs residents $104 per person per year; in Ireland, the Irish pay $71 per person per year for RTE.

Part of the problem with the CBC now is that Canadians take it for granted. The media landscape has changed drastically with the advent of online platforms. I learned about changing audiences and platforms when I taught my first class at UVic in 2012.

I hadn't been in this role before; I'd always been the student, not the teacher. My class was in a lecture hall with amphitheatre seat-ing. About sixty third-year journalism, history, and creative writ-ing students stared at me expectantly. After introducing myself, I asked, "How many of you listened to CBC Radio yesterday?"

Crickets. Not one student raised their hand. This was a class on public broadcasting, and no one listened to CBC. I then asked, "How many of you have a radio?" One brave student near the back raised her hand. This was going to be harder than I had imagined.

My next question received a more vigorous response and led to a fascinating discussion. "Where do you get your news?" The most common answer was "Facebook." This was 2012. Further discussion revealed that they followed Twitter, listened to podcasts, and listened to a digital version of CBC on their phones.

My first assignment for them was called "This Week Has Three Hours." I asked them to experience three distinct hours of CBC content over the next week on at least two different platforms; they couldn't watch a hockey game and call it a week. I asked them to keep a journal with observations about what they watched, listened to, or read.

Their responses were enlightening. The most common observation was, "I didn't know this was a CBC show." I read this from students who listened to *Quirks & Quarks*, the science show with Bob McDonald, and *The Vinyl Cafe* with Stuart McLean. They discovered *Little Mosque on the Prairie*, *Just for Laughs*, and *The Fifth Estate*. They also realized they were using the CBC website to follow news stories. And while most of them had seen my photo in an ad on the side of a bus or in a flyer for an event I was hosting, they hadn't previously tuned in to listen to me on *All Points West*.

Recently, I spoke to a former colleague who had just retired from the CBC and had been covering politics since 1988. (I am not using his name because he is not speaking on behalf of the corporation and would need official permission to comment; I have confirmed his observations with two other journalists who agreed he was accurate in his observations.) I asked him how covering politics has changed for journalists in the last twenty-five years.

He says there is incredible competition, with more political shows than ever. He says these shows are not doing just "news-release" journalism. There is a greater emphasis on enterprise reporting—finding out what is behind the news release and why something has happened, and there is no such thing as a radio reporter or a TV reporter anymore. Everyone has to be able to report on multiple platforms. A prediction made by a former CBC president Hubert Lacroix that CBC reporters would become "platform agnostic" has come true. My former colleague also points out that reporting can now be as immediate as "live tweeting" an event or as long-term as creating a podcast that takes six months.

He said what has changed is the need for fact-checking by both journalists and audiences. With so many platforms and aggregators providing news from various sources, false or incorrect news can take on a life of its own. More coverage of live events means political parties or groups can present their points of view without filters. He adds that politicians are much more controlled and scripted than in the past, and getting anyone to open up about what they really think is more challenging than ever.

He believes all this is leading to fracturing within Parliament and in media.

His words echoed in my ears when I heard the organizers of the Freedom Convoy announce they were not allowing CTV, CBC, and the *Toronto Star* to attend their first news conference. There was a time when, if a legitimate news organization was banned from a news conference, all other media would walk out in solidarity—as I experienced in 1980, when the outside workers, CUPE Local 18, were on strike in Saint John, NB.

It was a strike with lots of rhetoric and animosity. I was a CBC Radio reporter—a unionized position—assigned to cover the strike. To get an interview from management, it was necessary for me to cross a picket line. I spoke to the guys on the line and explained my situation. I had already interviewed the union boss and needed to go inside the building to hear from the other side. They let me pass. I filed my story.

Unfortunately, the CUPE Local union boss was unhappy that I had crossed the line. When I woke up the following day, I had two flat tires. They had been punctured. I got a ride to work and received a call from a colleague at another radio station. He wondered why I wasn't at the news conference. I told him I hadn't been told about it. He went into the news conference and asked the CUPE organizer if CBC Radio had been invited. He was told, "No, we don't want Jo-Ann Roberts at this news conference." The other news outlets' reporters stood up and said, "Then we're not staying." CUPE backed down. The news conference was rescheduled, and I was invited.

Now the media, much like society, is divided into conservative- and liberal-leaning news outlets, and they don't trust each other, let alone work together. News teams are overworked and under-staffed, and there is little time to take a stand on ethical issues that don't affect them directly.

On April 27, 2023, Bill C-11 updated the Broadcasting Act to reflect technologies like streaming services, internet video, and digital media. The review panel that advised the minister on this legis-lation called for the end of advertising on the CBC while recom-mending that streaming services like Netflix and Prime Video be mandated to fund the creation of Canadian content. The minister stopped short of ending advertising on the CBC.

In the interest of preserving an institution that is essential to democracy, it is time to rethink how we fund our public broad-caster. I support the move to eliminate advertising from television and online. This would mean that the public broadcaster is not in competition with private media companies for advertising dollars. As an additional source of revenue, private broadcasters could contract with the CBC to carry CBC news. A public broadcaster not tied to advertising could be an asset to journalists working for private outlets.

But it's problematic that the funding for the public broadcaster is tied to the annual federal government budget cycle. The solution lies in creating a funding model that is stable, long-term, and not tied to the election cycle. A model I believe could work—and benefit both journalism and democracy—would be to have fixed funding for at least five years supported by a tax on other media platforms like streaming services, video channels, and digital media, and reporting annually to an all-party committee of Parliament.

We know the power of the mass media. I knew it when I was twelve. It is time to ask ourselves what we value and put the necessary safeguards in place to ensure truth and democracy aren't lost in the fight for our hearts and minds.

VOTING REVOLUTION TIP

Call for fixed, stable funding for public broadcasting in Canada. A free press and public broadcasting are essential to a functional democracy. Voters can help by advocating for funding that is at arm's-length from partisan political and commercial interests and supported by a tax on other media platforms.

Canadians also need to support and protect journalism in the private sector in Canada by setting standards, creating funds to encourage the development of Canadian content, and holding all companies who wish to be in the Canadian marketplace to the same values. We have a very uneven playing field right now; no one is setting the rules or refereeing the match.

I learned on the asphalt playground at Prince Charles School that the world is tough; not everyone is going to play nice. But if we don't want the bullies to take over, we need the brave voices of those who will accurately report what they see to protect those who are working for the common good.

CHAPTER 4

MAKING VOTES COUNT

The Promise of Proportional Representation

ACKNOWLEDGE THAT MY PASSION FOR DEMOCRACY AND electoral reform is a bit niche and makes me something of a political nerd. But I'm not alone, and it is always rewarding when I meet like-minded people. Many of us democracy nerds want to see some form of proportional representation (PR) in Canada, in which each political party receives the number of seats in the House of Commons that's proportional to the percentage of votes the party earns in the election.

But no one has influenced me more in supporting that idea than Wendy Bergerud.

Wendy Bergerud showed up at my Victoria campaign office on St. Patrick's Day 2015—an auspicious day for Greens—to convince me to sign the Fair Vote Canada pledge. The daffodils were blooming when I promised that, if elected, I would change our electoral system to make every vote count.

Bergerud was a wife and mother who worked as a biometrician with the British Columbia Ministry of Forests. She had been forty-nine back in 2003 when she'd received one of 15,800 invitations sent out by the provincial government—200 in each constituency—asking if she was willing to put her name into a draw to serve on the BC Citizens' Assembly on Electoral Reform. She'd agreed, thinking, "Why not? This could be interesting." She was a passionate advocate for civic rights. By the end of that year, when the lottery process was over, she was one of the final 161 people who had been randomly selected for the assembly. Their job was to study electoral systems worldwide and recommend to the provincial government what they thought would be best for the province.

When I was the host for *All Points West* on CBC Radio, I had a chance to interview several members of the Citizens' Assembly in

BC. What struck me most was how well-informed they were after just three months of studying the question and hearing from experts from countries with some form of proportional representation.

These 161 citizens represented all British Columbians. The assembly was balanced along regional, gender, and age lines. It held over fifty public hearings and received 1,603 submissions from the public.

In 2004, the Citizens' Assembly made its recommendation to the government of British Columbia: the province should implement a single transferable vote (STV), which allows voters to rank their choices as first, second, and third. This system is used nationally in Ireland, in the Australian Capital Territory and Tasmania, and in Scotland for local elections.

But instead of implementing the system for at least one election cycle so the public could determine whether it worked, the government put it to a referendum during the 2005 provincial election. A super-majority was required for the proposal to pass, which meant approval by 60 percent of voters overall and a majority in 60 percent of the seventy-nine districts—setting the bar higher than the one politicians have to meet to get elected. In the end, seventy-seven of the districts supported the change, but the overall vote was 57.7 percent—falling short by only 2.3 percent.

Another referendum was held during the 2009 provincial election but, by that point, the momentum had been lost and the proposal received just 40 percent support.

———

Under Stephen Harper's leadership in 2011, the federal Conservatives were elected to a majority government—166 seats with 39.6 percent of the vote. Over the next four years, his government silenced scientists researching climate change, muzzled media coverage of the government, and eliminated the national census. These three issues alone worried a lot of citizens. In essence, the Conservative Party wielded 100 percent of the power, despite having earned fewer than 40 percent of the votes.

The Liberal Party had lost forty-three seats and was no longer the governing party or the Official Opposition. The Liberals had fallen to third-party status behind the NDP and, for the first time in the Liberal Party's history, were open to considering the value of electoral reform.

Additionally, the Green Party of Canada had experienced a breakthrough in 2011 when Elizabeth May was elected as the first Green MP in Canadian history. However, the Greens had also realized that, with almost 4 percent of the national vote, they would have had thirteen seats if proportional representation had been in place.

Bergerud and her colleagues had no idea at that point when they would get another chance at significant electoral reform, but the period leading up to the 2015 election had seemed like a perfect opportunity: many progressive voters were fed up with Stephen Harper's government. Bergerud and other members of Fair Vote Canada saw their opportunity and started campaigning hard to make electoral reform a ballot-box issue. They recruited candidates nationwide to take the pledge.

Liberals and New Democrats both pledged electoral reform during the 2015 election campaign. Three months after I signed my pledge, Liberal leader Justin Trudeau vowed that the upcoming general election would be the last one using the first-past-the-post system. (Green Party members would count the number of times he pledged that 2015 would be the last election under first-past-the-post: it came to more than 1,200!)

On that St. Paddy's Day 2015, I was sitting in the boardroom of our campaign office on Yates Street when Bergerud set up her flip chart to make her Fair Vote presentation. She was a couple of years older than me, of Nordic heritage, with dirty-blonde hair to her shoulders and a full, round face with rosy cheeks. She wore a Fair Vote Canada T-shirt and khaki pants. Her goal was to convince me nothing mattered more in this election than changing our electoral system.

She was passionate. Bergerud wanted to get every interested candidate to sign the pledge, but not until they understood what electoral reform meant and why it mattered. Even when I reminded her that electoral reform was part of the Green Party platform and that I could save her time and just sign the pledge, there was no stopping her. She wanted to ensure I was well-equipped to answer questions on the issue and hoped I would understand why she was so passionate. I worried she would make me take an exam before letting me sign the pledge! A couple of hours later I had signed, and Bergerud was on her way to convince another candidate of the value of her cause.

Once the writ was dropped and there were campaign events every day, Bergerud and I ran into each other often. She was usually handing out leaflets or getting voters to agree to vote for candidates who favoured proportional representation. She also helped organize debates on electoral reform. Bergerud was non-partisan; for her, this election was about one issue. Often, after an event, we would talk about why it was so important to her. She told me that being part of the Citizens' Assembly had changed the next decade of her life; it had convinced her that democracy could be better in Canada. She wanted every vote to count. I was always amazed at her dedication, despite the two major setbacks she and thousands of electoral reform campaigners in BC had faced in the previous two provincial elections.

In September, I noticed Bergerud looked tired and had lost some weight, but we were all tired. This had been the longest campaign in recent Canadian history and the battle was fast-paced and intense. Change was in the air. Many people told me on their doorsteps they wouldn't vote for me this time, but would be happy to vote for me once we had proportional representation. It was so frustrating! I assured them the best way to make sure we had proportional representation was to vote for me now so I could vote for it in the House of Commons, but many still felt they couldn't take the risk of voting for someone who might not win, because they didn't want to waste their vote.

This argument has haunted me and every Green Party candidate in every campaign I've worked on. When will voters finally realize it is a self-fulfilling prophecy, and that Greens will win when people vote Green?

The outcome of that election was very personal for me. I received 23,666 votes (33 percent of all the votes cast), but I lost, even though I received more votes than 131 MPs who actually won seats in that election. The winner, NDP candidate Murray Rankin, received 30,397 votes (42 percent of the votes cast). The leader of the NDP, Thomas Mulcair, was elected with just 19,242 votes. There was no way those who had voted for me could have their vote reflected in the representatives elected to the House of Commons. Quite simply, it was not fair.

Elizabeth May, the leader of the Green Party of Canada, was re-elected in 2015, but she was the only Green MP elected, even though 4 percent of all voters in Canada—602,933 people—voted Green. Compare this with the Bloc Québécois, who received 821,444 votes (4.6 percent of all votes cast) and won ten seats.

Just like Stephen Harper's Conservatives before him, Justin Trudeau's Liberals won a majority in the House of Commons and formed a government with 39 percent of the vote—and 100 percent of the power.

I saw Bergerud briefly right after the election. We both agreed the greatest outcome of this election was that, given the Liberals' campaign promises, there was now the real possibility of electoral reform, which would be good for democracy.

A few months went by. I was busy feeling sorry for myself when my husband was diagnosed with advanced prostate cancer. He had surgery a month later, in January 2016.

One day, near the end of February, I ran into a friend of Bergerud's at the hospital. I asked how she was. The friend replied with a worried expression, "You haven't heard? Wendy's cancer came back in September. She's here in the hospital, in palliative care. She doesn't have long."

I felt my knees go weak. All I could think was that she had been fighting cancer *while* fighting for proportional representation.

A couple of days later, I grabbed a bouquet of daffodils, her favourite flower, and went to see her. She was propped up in bed;

the sun shone through the window. She thanked me for the flowers and asked me to sign a notebook she kept by the bed so her family would know who had dropped by.

I didn't stay long. We didn't talk about the election; instead, we talked about our families and people we knew. As I prepared to leave, I thanked her for her passion and commitment to electoral reform. I told her it had made a difference to me. I assured her I would continue to fight for a better, fairer democracy, and that I was glad she had lived to see a government elected that would bring about electoral reform. We briefly discussed what it would mean for the next election and how exciting it would be.

I wept when I left the room—not because we had been close friends, but because she was such a strong, positive person who had fought hard for what she believed in. I admired her and knew we were losing her way too soon.

She died a week later—before seeing the daffodils bloom again.

Provinces including New Brunswick, Ontario, and Quebec have all shown interest in electoral reform in the past, but it hasn't happened. In New Brunswick, an eight-person Commission on Legislative Democracy was established in 2003. It released a report in 2005 endorsing a voting system called mixed member proportional (MMP), in which voters get two votes—one to decide on a representative for their district and one for a political party. The Progressive Conservative government of Bernard Lord promised to hold a referendum on reform in May 2008 but, as it turned out, Lord's government was defeated in the 2006 election and the referendum was never held.

Meanwhile, a Citizens' Assembly on Electoral Reform was formed in Ontario in 2006. In May 2007, they released a report endorsing MMP. A referendum was held on the proposal in October 2007; it required 60 percent support to pass, but failed, receiving only 37 percent. After the vote, Elections Ontario, the province's non-partisan agency responsible for the administration of elections, was criticized by politicians from all of the major parties for failing to adequately inform voters about the nature of the proposed reform.

Broadcaster Jo-Ann Roberts at the CBC-TV news desk covering the New Brunswick provincial election on June 9, 2003, with journalist Terry Seguin and political scientist Dr. Richard Sigurdson. [AUTHOR COLLECTION]

In Quebec, a citizens' committee released a report in April 2006 proposing a mixed member proportional voting system, but the government made no commitment to either implement the proposal or hold a referendum.

This pattern of introducing the concept of electoral reform and then finding ways to delay or defeat it is far too familiar. Prince Edward Island had attempted to implement electoral reform in 2005, holding a referendum on switching from first-past-the-post to a mixed member proportional system. The proposal received only 36 percent support, which many proponents of the reform claimed resulted from an insufficient public education campaign by Elections PEI.

An electoral reform referendum was held again in PEI in 2016. Interestingly, this referendum was introduced after provincial

Green Party Leader Peter Bevan-Baker won his seat, making him only the second third-party MP in PEI history to be elected to the legislature. The plebiscite ballot offered voters three forms of proportional representation plus the option to keep first-past-the-post. It was a preferential ballot, which meant voters could rank their choices.

The final vote was 52.4 percent in favour of MMP, with 42.8 percent in favour of keeping first-past-the-post. It was not a binding referendum, so despite most voters indicating they wanted a change, the premier, Wade MacLauchlan, questioned the validity of the results because there was a low voter turnout (36.46 percent) and declared another referendum would be held during the next provincial election in 2019.

The results of that referendum were close, but the reverse of 2016—51 percent in favour of keeping the old system and 49 percent in favour of adopting a new one. During that election, the Liberals lost their majority and Premier MacLauchlan lost his seat. While the Progressive Conservatives won the most seats, they did not have a majority. The Green Party of PEI became the Official Opposition with eight seats. The province's voters clearly wanted change, so what had prevented them from going all the way and changing their voting system?

A report by PEI's referendum commissioner Gerard Mitchell, who had been appointed to ensure the fairness of the vote, made some very astute observations about why the move to adopt MMP had failed. Mitchell said there was a fear in rural areas that they would not be as well represented under the new voting system. He also said voters needed to be clearer about details, such as how the system would avoid having single-issue candidates. He also pointed out that candidates had been prevented from campaigning on the referendum issue by the rules that had set up two official groups—one to represent each side. He said this resulted in too much time arguing about the rules around who could campaign when voters needed clarification on how the system would work. It's interesting to note that the very rules that were meant to keep the referendum non-partisan ended up preventing discussion about the system because candidates were forbidden from giving their opinions when they were knocking on doors.

Peter Bevan-Baker says he was so frustrated by the rules, and the fact that they seemed to muzzle candidates and political parties, that the Green Party of PEI considered launching a constitutional challenge to the legislation. In the end, they felt they were unlikely to get a decision in time to make a difference, and time and money are in short supply during an election. However, the tenacious Bevan-Baker is not a man who gives up quickly on what he believes in. He had run and lost in nine elections before finally being elected on his tenth attempt. As leader of the Official Opposition in PEI, he was optimistic that the Island could be the first province to introduce proportional representation.

Clearly, it's hard for voters to understand electoral reform without concrete experience—it's like learning to knit without needles and yarn. But it seems proportional representation is always moving two steps forward and three steps back. We know there's a problem with our electoral system or we wouldn't study it so much. Opposition parties favour electoral reform but lose their nerve when they're in power. Even when provincial election offices propose change, reform hits a brick wall once it lands on the legislature floor.

I haven't talked in great detail about how the different forms of proportional representation (PR) work. There's a reason for that. First-past-the-post is easy to explain and easy to understand. Voters are familiar with it. It's used in daily life; if a group is trying to decide whether to go to the movies or out to dinner, they just take a vote. Majority wins. This makes it easy to create a strategy to win. It's the devil we know.

First Past the Pizza

A YouTube video called "First Past the Pizza," which was produced as part of a competition for Fair Vote Canada, illustrates what's wrong with first-past-the-post voting. Here's the scenario:

Six friends attempt to order pizza; all want different toppings except two, who both want meat-lovers.

"Great, I'll get two meat-lovers," says the guy who's buying.

His friends protest. "That's not fair! Only two people are getting what they want."

His response: "That's too bad. We voted and meat-lovers won. That's how democracy works."

The friends point out that the second pizza could be split into thirds: ham and pineapple, vegetarian, bacon chicken.

"No," says the guy, "that would be too confusing. We're getting two meat lovers."

And that's how elections work in Canada.

Other ways of electing governments, such as single transferable vote or mixed member proportional, are more complicated. In a referendum, those who want to keep first-past-the-post spend a lot of time playing up the complexities of MMP or STV, and it's easy to get lost in the details. Voters sometimes throw up their hands and decide not to vote for any kind of PR because they don't fully understand how it works.

Opponents of electoral reform, like the guy in the pizza skit (see "First Past the Pizza" sidebar), say PR is complicated and confusing. Others worry a government elected under PR will be unstable and take longer to get things done. But I believe those arguments are simply a deflection from a political class that fears change.

Elizabeth May was, to put it mildly, discouraged by the results of the 2015 election. She had honestly hoped she would have company in Ottawa—particularly mine. We had dreamed of working together. I knew how disappointed I was, but I hadn't realized how hard my defeat would be for May. She had been invested in my campaign, and we had seen each other a lot on the campaign trail.

There was no time to grieve on election night. It took all the energy I had to be graceful in defeat. I stood on the stage to thank my supporters. I was wearing a new dress I'd bought earlier in the day—a lovely teal green in a festive fabric. My husband, all four kids, our daughter-in-law, and our seven-month-old granddaughter were all on the stage, standing behind me and supporting me as they had throughout the campaign. We even had Moses, our campaign dog, with us. They had all hoped, and probably believed, I would win. But I smiled, so they smiled. When I look at the pictures of us on the stage that night, we don't look like losers. In my speech, I said, "Don't be discouraged. The Liberals, led by Justin Trudeau, have promised this will be the last election run under first-past-the-post. That will make a difference. We will build on the support we have been shown tonight. We must see this as a win."

We know from the results in other countries that more Green Party candidates win under a proportional representation system. By 2015, only two Greens worldwide had ever been elected federally under the first-past-the-post system: Elizabeth May in Canada and Caroline Lucas of the Green Party of England and Wales. It was only slightly better at the provincial level in Canada, but at least there were some encouraging developments. Greens had recently

Green Party candidate Jo-Ann Roberts delivers her concession speech on October 19, 2015, at the Victoria Convention Centre in Victoria, BC, with family looking on. Behind her, from L: Ken Kelly, Alyson Kelly, Meghan Kelly, Christopher Kelly (holding Georgia), Lauren Bercovitch Kelly, and Claire Kelly. Moses the dog looks on mournfully. [The Canadian Press/Chad Hipolito]

been elected in three provinces: Andrew Weaver in BC in 2013; David Coon in NB in 2014; and Peter Bevan-Baker in PEI in 2015.

When the election was over, May was immediately off to the United Nations Climate Change Conference in Paris and when she returned, she was back to the gruelling pace of flying back and forth to Ottawa. In February 2016, she was back on Vancouver Island and asked a few of the 2015 candidates if we would like to gather with her for an early Valentine's Day dinner. I had always been in awe of Elizabeth May, but at that point I got to know her hopes, dreams, fears, and frailties. As we enjoyed sparkling wine and cheese and took in the view of the Salish Sea, I realized I may have lost an election, but I had gained a friend.

So it was hard to watch what happened next as my friend set out to salvage what she considered the one good thing that had come out of the election, aside from her re-election. She dedicated herself to ensuring that Canada had seen its last election under first-past-the-post. She was a long-time champion of electoral reform and an acknowledged expert on it from her years of work with Greens worldwide who had been elected under proportional representation voting systems.

May was an obvious choice for the House of Commons Special Committee on Electoral Reform (also known as the ERRE), which was empowered to "conduct a study of a viable alternate voting system to replace the first-past-the-post system, as well as to examine mandatory voting and online voting." When the makeup of the committee was announced on May 10, 2016, May was shocked to learn that she had been made a non-voting member. There were six Liberal members, three Conservatives, and one New Democrat—all voting members—and two non-voting members: Luc Thériault from the Bloc Québécois and Elizabeth May.

Rona Ambrose, the interim Conservative leader at the time, nailed it when she said the Liberals were "stacking the deck." Because May and the Bloc member were non-voting, the Liberals could recommend changes to the voting system—or not—without the support of any other party. In hindsight, maybe it should have been evident that the Liberals had no intention of making any changes to the voting system that didn't favour their party.

May was very public about how unfair it was to ask her to give her time and expertise to hearing from Canadians and then not allow her to vote on the recommendations. She had the support of NDP MP Nathan Cullen, who was also from BC. Finally, on June 2, 2016, the government relented, supporting a motion from Cullen that called for the committee's structure to be determined by the percentage of the nationwide popular vote each party had received in the previous election—PR in action. How appropriate! That meant only five Liberals on the committee, one of them the chair who could only vote in the case of a tie, three Conservatives, two New Democrats, one Green, and one Bloc. All were voting members—much more democratic.

The ERRE was to issue its report to the House of Commons no later than December 1, 2016. The first meeting was held on June 21; members met all summer and held public meetings in communities across Canada in September and October, where presentations were heard from numerous public servants, academics, members of the public, and electoral officers worldwide.

In September, May asked me to join her to attend a public meeting on Saturna Island, BC, with the minister of electoral reform, Maryam Monsef. I remember it well. It was so typical of politics, Saanich–Gulf Islands style. The day started with a ferry ride to the island: beautiful blue skies and passengers watching for whales. We arrived and immediately set out to meet up with Senator Pat Carney, a former Progressive Conservative MP and cabinet member, and a long-time friend of May's, who was living on Saturna Island. Senator Carney joined us at East Point, the Gulf Islands National Park reserve. Orcas often pass East Point on their way to and from the mouth of the Fraser River. We didn't see any whales on that day, but did see many sea lions. It was windy, so after a short hike around the property, we headed into a white saltbox cabin to learn more about the site. Minister Monsef joined us and discussed the importance of preserving our environment. I was struck by how quickly the political issues that divided these three mighty women—a Liberal, a Conservative, and a Green—had disappeared.

The next stop was a potluck meal at the community hall. The island is home to just 350 residents and, as we headed into the auditorium for the public meeting on electoral reform, it felt like they were all there. In reality, only about 100 people were in the room, but they were engaged and eager to hear what their MP and the minister had to say. May's passion was fully on display as she discussed how essential it was that we "grab this historic moment." A student of history, May said the issue had been studied by at least six task forces and committees, going as far back as 1921, and noted "not one of the studies suggested we keep first-past-the-post." I joined the enthusiastic applause. We believed we were part of history-in-the-making.

Monsef was eloquent and careful in her speech, advising the crowd not to judge the outcome of what the committee might recommend. But she, too, seemed to sense it could be the beginning of a historic change in Canada. "We are doing this not for us," she said, "but for our children and grandchildren. This is a golden opportunity."

Three months later, Monsef openly criticized the committee's final report, which recommended a national referendum on changing the voting system. On the floor of the House of Commons, she said, "They did not complete the hard work we had expected them to." She also said, "On the hard choices that we asked the committee to make, Mr. Speaker, they took a pass." It was a slap in the face. She apologized the next day, but it became evident that the prime minister and the Liberal Party were setting the stage to abandon the promise to enact electoral reform, like so many had before.

By February 2017, Maryam Monsef was no longer the minister responsible for electoral reform. Maybe she wasn't willing to deliver the death blow to PR, or perhaps the prime minister couldn't keep the person who had called the first-past-the-post system "antiquated" in that portfolio. The job fell to Karina Gould, who announced on February 1, 2017, that "electoral reform is no longer in my mandate."

A few days later, Gould said: "The first-past-the-post system may not be perfect—no electoral system is. But it has served this country for 150 years and advances several democratic values that Canadians hold dear, such as strong local representation, stability, and accountability." Gould said the decision to abandon the Liberal Party's commitment to implement a new electoral system was "difficult" but "responsible," citing a lack of consensus around the options.

After that statement, which killed any hope of electoral reform, Elizabeth May walked out of the House of Commons chamber and into the foyer to face reporters. She was visibly upset and struggled to maintain her composure. At one point, her voice trembled. I thought she was going to weep.

"I am more deeply shocked and betrayed by my government today than on any day of my adult life," she said. "And that's saying something."

She closed her eyes and paused briefly before saying she was mortified that the prime minister had chosen two young women in the cabinet, referring to Maryam Monsef and Karina Gould, to bear the face of this betrayal.

"He threw them under the bus and left them to twist in the wind over his broken promise."

I knew, watching that media scrum, that my friend was devastated, and I was worried for her. She had campaigned throughout the summer of 2015, criss-crossing the country, not taking a break. She had been hoping she would be able to relax for a few weeks the following summer. Instead, she dedicated her time after the parliamentary session to hear witnesses and experts on democratic reform. She was tired, and while she had known there wouldn't be a simple way to move forward with proportional representation, she had been fuelled by the hope that the process would succeed this time. "I was expecting something, not nothing," she admitted. "It was embedded in the Speech from the Throne."

Jo-Ann Roberts (centre) at an Ottawa press gallery dinner at the Hull Museum of Civilization on May 26, 2018, with member of Parliament and national Green Party leader Elizabeth May (L) and May's parliamentary chief of staff, Debra Eindiguer.
[AUTHOR COLLECTION]

In addition to my concern for May, my thoughts turned to Wendy Bergerud. I was angry at the Liberals for betraying her and me and everyone who had honestly believed it was time to find a way to make every vote count.

I shouldn't have been surprised. Maybe Bergerud wouldn't have been either. No government in Canada has changed the system that has elected them, despite what they say before they are elected—and it's obvious why. Changing the system that put them in power isn't to their advantage; it works for them.

For May, it was a betrayal that led to a fundamental shift in her usually spirited approach to politics. Her trust had been shaken, not just in Justin Trudeau and the Liberal Party, but in politics and people.

She didn't quit; she's a fighter, but her hopes of building a coalition of like-minded politicians who would work to tackle climate change were shattered. She had believed that, with electoral reform, she could see a way forward; there was hope that more Green MPs would be elected and that politicians from all political parties would have more reason to work together. While hope wasn't entirely lost under first-past-the-post, it would be so much harder and take so much more time.

The backpedalling on electoral reform after the 2015 election undermined Canadian democracy in a way that wasn't obvious at the time.

Non-partisan third-party groups like Leadnow and Fair Vote Canada had actively encouraged people to vote Liberal because the Liberals were promising electoral reform and had the best chance of forming a government. The argument was: vote strategically now, and you will never have to vote strategically again because we will have proportional representation. I heard it on so many doorsteps.

What happens when governments break election promises without real justification? Cynicism grows. Voters lose faith in the system. They lose faith that their vote matters. They don't think they have any say, so they look for other ways to be heard.

The seeds of the Freedom Convoy may be traceable to seeds planted during the abandonment of Trudeau's promise for electoral reform. While, on the surface, the convoy was about opposition to vaccine mandates for cross-border truck drivers, Canada Unity, one of the groups behind the organization of the Freedom Convoy, had a much broader goal. In a manifesto published a month *before* the vaccination mandate for cross-border truckers was announced, Canada Unity said it wanted the unelected Senate and the governor-general to dissolve Parliament and, with their help, take over the government. Canada Unity's website (which is no longer functioning) accused Justin Trudeau and the Liberals of "stealing" elections. Much of the information on the site was inflammatory, but some of the elements of what they stood for might appeal to those who felt left behind—and unheard—by a progressive, diverse, and changing society.

It's true that politics in Canada doesn't allow for a diversity of voices. For any group to have power, they have to be part of one of the two major parties: the Liberals or the Conservatives. But Canadians are not split down the middle, left and right, Liberal or Conservative. We have progressive NDP voices, environmental Green voices, nationalist Bloc Québécois voices, People's Party of Canada voices, and even Freedom Convoy voices. Under first-past-the-post, none of these voices are heard.

We should be troubled that one-third of eligible voters in Canada are just not voting—it's a response to a voting system that does not encourage a diversity of viewpoints or cooperation and compromise across the political spectrum. Our first-past-the-post voting system was designed for a country with two parties. Canada has outgrown that system.

Here's what I propose: first, we ask voters—through a referendum—if they want electoral reform, period. If a majority says yes, then we hold at least one election under whatever system a Citizens' Assembly recommends. Voters can learn through that election how PR works. Follow that up with another referendum to determine whether voters want to keep that system.

Wendy Bergerud's last dozen years had been dedicated to an important cause—advocating for proportional representation. What would Bergerud say to me now? She knew what every committee, commission, and citizens' assembly from 1921 to 2016 had recommended: there is a better way. Bergerud would want me to look at the beautiful daffodils that build their strength in the dark of winter so they can bloom in the spring—and remember that this is worth fighting for.

Democracy demands it.

VOTING REVOLUTION TIP

Work toward proportional representation: collectively agree to try some form of electoral reform in the next election cycle and hold a federal referendum on electoral reform. If a majority favours PR, have a Citizens' Assembly recommend a system; hold at least one election under that system. Follow up with another referendum to determine whether voters want to keep that system.

CHAPTER 5

FUTURE PRESENT

On the Importance of Raising Young Voters

IN AN EFFORT TO ENCOURAGE PEOPLE TO VOTE AND, IN particular, to vote for them, most candidates spend a fair amount of time knocking on doors. That often leads to some...shall we say... interesting stories about those experiences. Here's just one of mine.

It's September 2015, a warm Saturday afternoon in Victoria. I'm out with a new volunteer, a woman a little younger than me. We're getting to know each other, chatting between doorsteps. I'm knocking; she's writing notes. We get into a rhythm: grab a brochure, knock on the door, leave a note; brochure, knock, note; brochure, knock, note. Many people are not at home, but we remind ourselves that this is the hard work that wins elections.

It's a working-class neighbourhood with lots of kids and dogs. Most people here are renters. It's a treat when we find someone who's home and wants to talk. We have a great conversation with a couple living in the house on the corner. They invite us into their garden and are interested in voting Green. When they say they'll take a regular lawn sign, we're excited; this is a good location. We might even convince them to upgrade to a big sign.

The next address on our map is across the street. I climb the concrete steps of the light-blue bungalow. The landing is very small; the screen door is weathered. There is no garden or landscaping at this address. Our list from Elections Canada says two voters live in the house; based on the names, it's probably a couple or a mother and son. There is no doorbell, so I knock, gripping my campaign flyer, which is like a long postcard with a big picture of me on the front and some info on why I'm running on the back. I'm about to write "Sorry I missed you" on the postcard and leave it in the mailbox when the door is flung open.

I step back and stammer, "Hello...hi...I'm...Jo-Ann Roberts."

I try not to stare. A young man's massive body fills the doorway. He has wavy brown hair down to his shoulders, and he's stark naked. Or at least, I think he's stark naked; his massive belly is making it impossible to tell if he's wearing briefs.

I go on autopilot, still talking and trying to figure out what to do next. My mind is racing as I begin to process the enormous tattoo stretching like a billboard from one shoulder to the other across his chest. It's in an Old English font; each letter is about six inches high.

I must have finally stopped talking because he speaks. "I don't want your brochure. I don't vote."

"Why not?" I ask. "This is an important election; maybe I can give you a reason to vote now."

"I don't vote," he says, slamming the door.

That's when the tattoo registers: "Mama's Boy."

I didn't have a chance to ask Mama's Boy if his mother was home or if she was a voter. I wish I had.

I've never forgotten Mama's Boy. His image comes to mind whenever I wonder why people don't vote. I'm not sure what his reasons were, but I know he's not alone. As I've mentioned before, eleven million Canadians don't vote.

Mama's Boy fits the profile of the largest group of non-voters. He's male and between the ages of eighteen and thirty-four. Other indicators that a person is unlikely to vote are that they do not have a university degree or they have a very low income.

When Elections Canada asked Canadians why they hadn't been voting for several years, the top reason was "not interested in politics." So let's turn the question on its head and ask, "Why do Canadians vote?"—particularly Canadians who are eighteen to thirty-four.

How do you raise a voter? I have four children; their levels of political activity vary. In essence, I have a built-in focus group for this question.

One has been a Green Party candidate federally and provincially. The others have worked on campaigns—mine and their sister's. All of them can hold their own in animated family political debates. They all agree that it makes a difference to have met politicians, which demonstrates that these are real people, not just faces on posters or on TV.

Our son, Chris, has a degree in theatre and made a name for himself by creating a satiric CBC Radio show called *This is That*. The show ran for seven years and was an award-winning podcast. He also won an international award for a comedy video he made for the *New York Times* which lampoons gun laws in the United States. I'm pretty sure he votes, but he's unlikely to put his name on a ballot as a candidate, so I asked him if he was political. His answer was as subtle as his satire.

"I think my work makes a political statement without being obviously political."

He remembers meeting Claudette Bradshaw when he was in high school. At the time, we lived in Riverview, NB, and Claudette was the MP for our riding, Moncton–Riverview–Dieppe. Claudette was a Liberal and a federal cabinet minister. She was very down-to-earth—an Acadian with a husky smoker's voice who was known for her fabulous hugs. I knew Claudette because my father helped her create Moncton Headstart in 1974. Headstart began as a modest childcare program that offered free daycare for economically disadvantaged children to help prepare them for grade 1. Today, it provides a wide range of services to support vulnerable, at-risk children and their families.

At that time—1998—I was the host of CBC's *Information Morning* in Moncton. I interviewed Claudette often, first in her role with Headstart and then as the MP for the riding. We had a connection beyond the CBC because of my dad, so whenever we met in town, she would always stop to chat.

Headstart had a turkey drive at Christmastime and would prepare Christmas hampers for disadvantaged families. One year, our whole family piled into our trusty blue Ford Windstar van and headed to the Moncton Coliseum to help deliver the hampers. It was a drive-through operation. We drove up, opened the back, someone put in half a dozen boxes and handed us the addresses for delivery. Claudette was in her parka, waving at people she knew and helping with boxes. When we picked up ours, she came over to the van, reached in for a big hug through the window, and said hi to all the kids. She thanked them for helping and wished them Merry Christmas—a natural politician; a person who cared about kids and Christmas was willing to stand out in a freezing parking lot and help load boxes.

When I asked Chris about it years later, he told me, "It was obvious Claudette was a person you admired because you said she was making a difference in people's lives. At the time, I thought you were referring to the Christmas hampers. It was much more than that, but it made a lasting impression. I couldn't vote in the federal election in 2000; it was two days before my eighteenth birthday. But when I finally got to vote in 2004, I voted for Claudette. I've voted in every federal election since."

Our middle daughter, Alyson, reminded me that much of her early political experience came by way of the school system. When she was in grade 6, her class held a mock election. She took on the role of Alexa McDonough, the leader of the federal NDP. She says she remembers researching McDonough and making a speech—and winning the election. Later that summer, she had a chance to meet McDonough on a beach in PEI. McDonough took the time to talk to Alyson and congratulated her when she heard about her classroom win. Alyson said what McDonough did for her was to reinforce the idea that women have an essential role in politics.

She says her political awakening came in grade 11 when she was chosen to participate in a French-language model parliament in Victoria, BC.

"We were actually in the legislature, sitting in the very seats the MLAs sit in. I had a chance to stand and make an amendment to a law that was being passed. The red carpet, the marble pillars, and the Speaker's chair all made an impression. I felt the reality of what a politician represents," she said. "I realized who gets to sit in these chairs is important; I think of that when I vote."

Alyson applied to be a page in the House of Commons the following year. She made it to the last round of the competition but didn't get the chance to serve in Ottawa. She is now a film producer, a mother, and a teacher living in rural Nova Scotia. She informed me the other day she is lobbying for safety upgrades to the road in front of her home and is considering running to be a member of her local village commission.

Our oldest daughter, Claire, has been a champion of social justice her entire life. She is in her thirties and has already run for office twice as a Green Party candidate—once federally and once provincially. After the federal campaign, she co-founded Femmocracy Now, a non-profit, non-partisan, bilingual group in Moncton, NB. Claire explains its mission is to amplify female voices in all spheres of power including politics, media, the economy, and the environment. Claire is a justice warrior and says she and the other members of Femmocracy Now realize men have a support network that does not exist in the same way for women. She hopes her organization will help address this need. She has a master's degree in immigration and settlement, has been an environmental activist since high school, and has a knack for languages. She is bilingual in French and English, speaks some

Japanese—she taught in Japan for two years—and is studying Mi'kmaq and Spanish, her husband's first language.

I was interested to find out what she thought had helped form her political activism.

"I remember we could never have a political sign on our lawn because you worked for the CBC and Dad worked for the town. We talked about politics and political issues at home, but we all knew you couldn't have a public opinion," she said. "The best thing about you becoming a candidate in 2015 is you were allowed to have opinions, and you could use a megaphone to talk about them."

A minor incident when Claire was about six years old gave me an early indication of the determined justice warrior she would become. We had gone to a Tim Hortons coffee shop for a donut. This was back when each Tim's had a glassed-in smoking area where hard-core smokers were on display.

"Why are all those people smoking?" Claire asked. "Don't they know that smoking could kill them?" I explained that it was hard to quit smoking and that they probably knew it was bad for them.

"I think we should tell them they shouldn't smoke," she insisted. Now she had my attention; this could be embarrassing. I explained to Claire that it might hurt someone's feelings if she said that to them and figured the case was closed. As we were heading back to the car, little Claire, with her big brown eyes and cute little Dorothy Hamill wedge haircut, saw a man coming out of the smoking room.

She stopped. "Sir, you shouldn't smoke. Smoking can kill you," she said loudly.

I was about to die of embarrassment when he replied, "Thanks for the advice. I've been thinking of quitting. It's a filthy habit. Don't ever start."

Claire seemed pretty pleased with herself as we climbed into the van.

In grade 5, Claire was one of the winners of an essay contest on the topic: "What I would do if I were mayor for a day." She didn't win the top prize of becoming the mayor, but she was a runner-up, and so became a councillor. She remembers there were only two girls on the council of eight. "I knew at the time there was something wrong with that."

Despite her passion for improving the world, Claire says she didn't think she would ever go into politics. She ran for "school spirit convenor" in grade 10, lost, and figured she would never run for anything again. Luckily, as Claire likes to say, "life doesn't end in high school."

She says reading the story of Anne Frank in junior high changed her view of the world.

"That book is the reason I do the work I do. I thought, 'How could humanity be so cruel? What's the basis of that?' That's why I studied social psychology," she said. "When I was studying the bystander effect, I realized there is less likelihood that someone will help if there is a large group until someone steps forward and changes things. I want to be the person who steps in to help when something wrong is happening."

Claire says she doesn't fault people for not voting.

"In our democracy, the only way to participate is by voting, and many people feel the system is out of their control. They feel disenfranchised by democracy. Our system needs to become more participatory," she says. "It's small, but I am impressed when elected officials hold regular town halls. They need to hear what people think and what matters to them. We need more opportunities for people to be heard, not just during an election campaign."

Our youngest, Meghan, is an artist who lived for almost a decade in New York and who now lives in Dublin, Ireland. She has done very well as a creative talent manager for tech companies, and she continues to paint on a commission basis.

I wasn't sure what she would say about politics. I began by asking her if she votes. She was adamant when she replied, "Of course I vote! I vote by mail. I think democracy is so important; we should not take it for granted. It sucks that I can't vote here, where I live, work, and pay taxes. I think people who can vote should vote."

I've always wondered why Meghan had been drawn to live and work in the United States. She surprised me when she explained how American politics had influenced her when she was growing up. She says she remembered all the talk about the controversial Bush–Gore election in 2000. She said it seemed to her that American politics was like a movie—much more interesting than Canadian politics. We moved to Victoria, BC, in 2004, when Meg was in grade 8. On a family trip to California, she bought a poster of Barack Obama, who had just been elected to the Senate. Then, in 2008, she bought one of the now-famous Obama "Hope" posters when he ran for president.

"I remember the day of Obama's inauguration," she told me. "Our teacher brought a TV into our classroom so we could watch his speech. I was so impressed by it. It felt like this was an historic moment. I think that was a pivotal moment for me."

She told me a person can't help but be aware of politics when they are living on a visa in another country. "The government can decide whether you can work or not—or come back into the country when you leave to visit family or go on vacation. During the Trump administration, I felt a great fear of ending up on a blacklist."

She said that because of her interest in art, she was influenced by the fashion styles of politicians.

"I remember you bought me a suit to wear to a wedding when I was twelve," she said. "You said it was a Jackie Kennedy Onassis–style suit. I remember I looked up her influence on fashion and started designing clothes like that, with pillbox hats and everything. I liked the poster art and loved studying the semiotics of campaign materials and what the symbols said about the campaign. Someday, I would like to work on a campaign."

She added, "I'm very proud of you, Mom."

And what about me? Hearing my kids' stories brought back memories of my own childhood.

My father was a United Church minister; he was brilliant and, in addition to his degree in theology, he had science and engineering degrees. He was tall, dark, and handsome, and in my mind, he could walk on water. I wanted to be just like him. I remember a particular moment in 1968: I was in grade 6 and we were living in Charlottetown, PEI. It was a Saturday, a bit cool, but all the snow was gone. Usually, I would have been out riding my bike with my friends, but on this day, I was inside watching TV with my dad, who was caught up in the Liberal leadership convention. The Liberals were choosing a successor for Lester B. Pearson.

Dad thought it was important—so I did, too.

There were some big names in the race in addition to Pierre Trudeau, who would eventually be chosen as the winner. On the ballot were Allan J. MacEachen, from Cape Breton; John Turner, who would briefly become prime minister in 1984; Paul Hellyer, who would go on to start his own short-lived political party called Action Canada; Paul Martin Sr., whose namesake son became prime minister from 2003 to 2006; Joe Greene, the minister of agriculture; Quebec politician Eric Kierans, who would become a popular panellist on *Morningside* with Peter Gzowski on CBC Radio; and my father's favourite candidate, Robert Winters, Pearson's minister of trade and commerce, originally from Lunenburg, NS.

There were four ballots stretched over seven and a half hours, all live on TV. It was better than a hockey game—and my dad and I loved to watch hockey. My father explained that he had backed Mitchell Sharp, but Sharp had pulled out of the race a couple of days before the convention and thrown his support behind Trudeau. Dad thought Trudeau was too young, so he was backing Bob Winters. I remember the drama when "Allan J.," along with Kierans and Martin, pulled out of the race. Martin and Kierans didn't support any other candidates. MacEachen threw his support behind Trudeau, but he was late withdrawing his name and declaring his support, and his name ended up on the second ballot.

When they announced the second ballot results, Trudeau was still in the lead, but he didn't have enough to win. Dad was excited because Bob Winters was in second, not Paul Hellyer, who had been expected to challenge Trudeau. Dad was excited and cheering. It was like we were sitting behind the bench at a hockey game. By the third ballot, I started to secretly cheer for Trudeau. I thought he was young and hip, compared to Bob Winters. There were lots of men in the Winters camp—some, like my dad, smoking pipes. The Trudeau team included women in their twenties wearing mini-skirts and go-go boots.

My father and I ate our dinner on TV trays as we waited for the fourth ballot. The game was going into overtime. I was beyond excited when Trudeau won. My dad was disappointed but impressed with Trudeau's acceptance speech, in which he called for Canada to be a "just society." By the end of the convention, I was completely enveloped by "Trudeaumania." My Dad must have been won over as well because, when it was announced that Pierre Trudeau was making a stop in Charlottetown and I begged to be allowed to go, Dad agreed I could miss school and join the crowds to see Trudeau downtown.

Prime Minister Pierre Trudeau, December 1975.
[WIKIMEDIA COMMONS]

The highlight of the rally for twelve-year-old me was when the very sexy Trudeau shook my hand. The rest of the world may have had the Rolling Stones or the Beatles, but the Stones didn't come to sleepy little Charlottetown. Pierre Elliot Trudeau was my rock star.

Politics was exciting.

Clearly, if we want to raise good citizens who vote, it helps to have a home where children can hear and participate in political discussions. But just as home is the ideal place to discuss sex and moral values, it should not be the only place where they are discussed.

Schools matter. What they teach matters, and I believe schools have a responsibility to teach how democracy works in Canada.

During my election campaigns, I have had the chance to speak at numerous schools. I never turn down a school invitation, but some candidates do. The reason may be obvious—kids don't vote. With limited time, candidates devote their energy to recruiting and identifying voters. While students might go home and tell their parents they are interested in a particular party or candidate, in the end, they won't be the ones marking the ballot.

But what if we changed that by lowering the voting age to sixteen? Promising research shows that if a person votes in the first election they are eligible for, they are more likely to vote in every election following.

The argument is often made that sixteen-year-olds are too young and can be too easily influenced by their peers or other forces. That makes me laugh because I know the flimsy reasons and weak rationale for voting many adults give me on the doorstep. The

Voting revolutionary Jo-Ann Roberts with a bullhorn, September 8, 2018, at a rally called "Rise for Climate to Build a Fossil-Free World" at the Halifax waterfront. [KEN KELLY]

Advocate to lower the voting age to sixteen and make civics education about elections and democracy mandatory in schools. We've already lowered the age from twenty-one to eighteen; we can take the next step. Young people are passionate and engaged and care about the important issues of the day. Also: promise to raise voters and talk about politics in a civilized manner!

truth is that we allow sixteen-year-olds to drive and join the Armed Forces—and we provide them with proper training to do these. The same should be true for voting.

If sixteen-year-olds could vote, there would be a solid reason to have high-quality, mandatory civic education in schools. Civic education programs do exist and are making a difference. Student Vote Canada is a learning program that collaborates with Elections Canada to provide students with the opportunity to experience the voting process first-hand.

In the 2019 federal election, student votes were held in eight thousand schools, representing all 338 federal electoral districts (since increased to 343 seats). Over a million students voted. The results were fascinating. The Liberals won 109 seats—fewer than the 157 they won at the national polls. The NDP won 101 seats, many more than the 24 they actually won at the polls. The Conservatives won 92 seats, compared to 121. The Bloc won 12 seats, compared to 32, and the Greens won 27, many more than the 3 they won on election night. Imagine what that Parliament would have been like.

The students cast their votes after learning about democracy and elections, researching the parties and platforms, and debating the country's future. They voted for the official candidates who were running in their districts. I applaud these students, their teachers, and this program.

But in 2020, Canada had 14,600 public schools. More than a third of them didn't take part in this program. At the very minimum, Student Vote should be a mandatory part of the curriculum during every federal election period.

———

I had a personal experience with the Student Vote program in 2019 and I'm certain it created two future voters.

The Green Party campaign office in Halifax in 2019 was impossible to miss. It was at the corner of two busy streets, Robie and Quinpool, across from the Halifax Commons; the exterior was painted a vivid green. Our entrance was next to a bus stop, and we kept the front doors open, weather permitting. Inside, it was a hive of activity. We had made a conscious decision to make it a place where people felt welcome. There were bowls of fresh fruit, muffins, fresh coffee, and at lunchtime, hot soup. Some volunteers came just for the soup, but it didn't matter; we were there to make politics accessible.

One day, two boys appeared in the office. They were brothers—Aaron and David.

"Hi! what brings you to our office?" I asked.

Aaron, the older one, said, "My teacher said we should check out who's running in this election. I look after my brother after school. On our way home we walk by this office, so we thought we'd drop in." I asked if their parents would be worried if they came home from school late. Aaron assured me he was in charge until his mom and dad came home from work, and it was okay to do this because it was homework. I gave him a tour of our space and gave them some buttons, stickers, and brochures. We had cookies and juice, and they left. I assumed that would be the last I would see of them.

Two days later, they came back. "We dropped in at the Liberal and Conservative offices," they said. Both of those campaign headquarters were also on our street.

"Could we come back here after school some days?" they asked.

"Of course!" I said. "Anytime." They came back two or three times a week, had a snack, helped with a few projects, stayed about half an hour, and then went on their way.

Then, the week before election day, I was at a school event at Gorsebrook Junior High in Halifax's south end. All of the students were gathered, seated on the floor in the school gym. I was there with the Liberal and NDP candidates—once again, the Conservative was a no-show.

It was noisy. A teacher raised her hand, and the kids were suddenly quiet. She then introduced the Liberal candidate, and there was a polite round of applause. He spoke for a few minutes. The same happened with the NDP candidate. When it was my turn, I was introduced, and there was a huge cheer and a round of sustained applause. The other candidates laughed. I was surprised. I spoke, and then we all answered prepared questions that students read. When it was time to leave, we left the gym ahead of the students, and then they filled the hallway, heading back to their classrooms. Suddenly, a group of boys was waving my Vote for Jo-Ann window signs. Aaron was the leader of the pack. He ran to me.

"I've been telling them all about you," he said. "And I gave them the buttons and the signs." He looked so proud and happy.

I won the Student Vote at Gorsebrook School in 2019. It was close—eighty-eight votes for me, seventy-three for the Liberal candidate. I have Aaron to thank for my victory.

Perhaps we're starting to see a theme here: politicians must be more visible and accessible. They need to go to schools and hold public town halls for all voters, not just the ones who will donate to their next campaign. There must be a connection between our elected officials and our daily lives.

Before the election was called in 2015, I was invited to speak to a grade 12 class in Victoria. The class was informal; students were seated on folding chairs in a circle. When the teacher introduced me, the kids were much more interested in my previous career as a radio host than in my desire to be an MP. In an attempt to engage them, I asked, "Is there anything you think your MP could do that would make a difference in your life?"

They stared at me, frozen, silent.

I was bombing. Finally, one skinny guy with black hair to his shoulders and a bit of casual confidence broke the sound barrier and replied, "Nope, I don't think anything an MP does affects me." I thanked him for answering and then had a brilliant idea. I asked, "How many of you have a cellphone?" Most of them put up their hands. I explained that their MP and the other MPs in the House of Commons made the rules for cellphones and controlled how phone plans operated. That got their attention. I told them the government also sets the voting age and asked them if they thought it would make a difference if they could vote at age sixteen. Suddenly, we were having a lively discussion.

Several groups are making the case for lowering the voting age to sixteen. A group of young Canadians has launched a court challenge to lower Canada's minimum age for voting in federal elections. In 2021, thirteen young people, including Amelia Penney-Crocker from Nova Scotia, filed an application at the Ontario Superior Court of Justice arguing that the section of the Canada Elections Act that bars Canadians under eighteen from voting in federal elections is unconstitutional.

The group argues that the rule violates two sections of the *Charter of Rights and Freedoms*: Section 3, which states that "every citizen of Canada" has the right to vote in an election for members of the House of Commons or a legislative assembly, and Section 15, which states that "every individual is equal before and under the law." The case is still making its way through the court system.

This may sound cynical, but I have witnessed the reality that not all politicians want more Canadians to vote.

One of the reasons there is resistance to lowering the voting age to sixteen is that no one can be sure how sixteen- and seventeen-year-olds might vote. Political parties work hard to understand their base—the people they can count on to vote for them. The major parties want *their supporters* to vote. Every party wants undecided voters to vote for them, but there isn't a huge push to get a massive turnout at the polls because it terrifies political parties to think of millions of non-voters or new voters exercising their franchise—it would change the dynamic, and quite possibly the election results.

In 2019, NDP MP Taylor Bachrach introduced a private member's bill to lower the voting age. It mirrors one in the Canadian Senate sponsored by Senator Marilou McPhedran. So far, none of these have succeeded, but it is time for a government to be bold and make this change.

One of the keys to getting voters of all ages engaged is to make politics more exciting. Just as Trudeaumania caught my attention in 1968—and the turnout of first-time voters reached a record high of 71 percent—Justin Trudeau caught the attention of younger voters in 2015, when first-time voters reached a turnout of 58 percent—a 20 percent increase over 2011. It helped that he was good-looking, but he was also relatable—a teacher who understood the power of the selfie.

A story Claire told me brings this full circle. During the 2019 campaign, the Liberal and Conservative campaigns called Claire's Green Party office and suggested that all three agree not to attend schools as part of the Student Vote initiative since there were no votes to be won in the schools and it took up valuable time that could be spent knocking on doors. Claire refused, so the only candidates who opted to go to the schools were the Greens, the NDP, the People's Party, and the Animal Protection Party. The English schools decided to go ahead without the Liberals and the Conservatives; the francophone schools cancelled the Student Vote event because the Liberals and Conservatives would not attend. Claire won the student vote in her riding over her primary opponent, the incumbent MP, who was a Liberal cabinet minister.

Near the end of the campaign, Claire and the other candidates were invited to literally "get in the ring" by participating in a wrestling event in Moncton. Claire agreed. She said it was fun and brought the election directly to wrestling fans.

When the fun match—complete with trash-talking—was over, Claire was approached by a young girl and her father. "My daughter saw you at her school and wants to tell you something," said the father.

"We had a vote in our classroom at school," she told Claire. "I was you. And guess what? I won!"

CHAPTER 6

CONTROLLING THE NARRATIVE

If You Don't, Others Will

THE SETTING IS THE WEST BLOCK OF THE PARLIAMENT buildings, September 12, 2022—two days after Pierre Poilievre's election as leader of the Conservative Party of Canada. It's his first news conference as leader of the Official Opposition. For the members of the Parliamentary Press Gallery, this event is like hundreds they have attended in their careers. However, this one will be remembered by everyone in attendance—and by the thousands who will watch it later on YouTube.

It will establish a narrative that will influence the next federal election.

Pierre Poilievre is holding a scrum—a media briefing—in the Foyer of the House of Commons. It's a backdrop well known to anyone with an interest in politics. A podium, a microphone, and large TV lights are permanently set up in the space. He's standing between the two Canadian flags that flank the mahogany doors behind him. Life-sized portraits of former Canadian prime ministers—including Sir Robert Borden and William Lyon Mackenzie King—line the stone walls. The members of the Parliamentary Press Gallery stand with microphones and cameras; reporters jostle for position. Scrums like these are much less formal than news conferences, which are held in the National Press Theatre or the Press Conference Room operated by the Press Gallery. The Foyer is often used for breaking news or to give members of the media an opportunity to ask questions about an evolving topic.

For anyone who happens to be watching this event live on CPAC (the Canadian TV network that presents parliamentary, political, and public affairs programming), what they see is not that unusual. Poilievre begins to speak then has an exchange with an off-screen reporter over whether he is going to take questions. Poilievre says, "I'm going to begin my remarks now." He tries to talk over the reporter, who keeps interrupting and throwing the Opposition Leader off his stride. Poilievre says he is being "heckled" by a "Liberal heckler." The reporter, David Akin, explains that he is the chief political correspondent for Global News. On CPAC, viewers can't see the reporter, but Poilievre is obviously annoyed.

It's difficult to hear the reporter when he says, "I have my hand up."

Poilievre shoots back: "What we have here is basically a Liberal heckler who snuck in here today."

Finally, after about two minutes of this back-and-forth, Poilievre agrees to take two questions at the end of his prepared remarks. Then he says, "I am going to start again...I want to speak directly to Canadians." He knows this is being carried live and will be recorded for anyone who wants to watch it later.

The news conference continues for another ten minutes. Poilievre stays on message, even when asked about a Conservative MP from Quebec who has left the caucus over Poilievre's leadership. His message is that inflation is the fault of government overspending. He refers to it several times in French and English as "JustinFlation," a play on words based on the prime minister's name. He takes two questions, as promised, neither of them from David Akin, and the scrum ends as he delivers the last word in his answer to the second question. He leaves the space, accompanied by his staff, while the reporters shout questions.

If someone had only seen this exchange on CPAC, it's unlikely they would have thought it was anything more than a feisty exchange between a politician and a reporter, which is certainly nothing new. But this exchange became the news of the day within hours.

A bit of background can help provide some context. The day before this event, Pierre Poilievre addressed his caucus; reporters were allowed to record the speech, but they were told to leave the room without asking questions. When the Press Gallery was told the following day that Poilievre would make an on-camera statement about inflation in the Foyer, they were again told he would not be taking any questions. Like most reporters, Akin, who has covered numerous federal elections, could see a pattern of stifling the media developing and wanted to nip it in the bud. He later conceded that he could have found another way to make his point. He apologized a few hours later on Twitter.

"Lots of readers/viewers called me about today's Parliament Hill presser," he wrote. "Many said I was rude and disrespectful to @ PierrePoilievre. I agree. I'm sorry for that. We all want politicians to answer questions—but there are better ways of making a point."

Meanwhile, about an hour after the event in the Foyer, Pierre Poilievre sent a letter to all Conservative Party members which described the event like this:

You won't believe this. I couldn't believe it, and it happened to me.

Today, I was delivering a statement about how Trudeau's inflation is hurting everyday Canadians when someone started shouting.

First, they hurled obscenities and then started shouting at me.

Was it some left-wing protestor? Maybe it was a Liberal MP or staffer?

No, it was a member of the media.

That's right. David Akin from Global News was swearing, shouting, and heckling. He wasn't interested in hearing what I had to say, and he certainly wasn't interested in reporting it in an unbiased way.

This is what we are up against.

It's not just the Liberals with all the advantages and resources of the federal government at their disposal.

It's the media, who are no longer interested in even pretending to be unbiased. They want us to lose.

But we have a secret weapon.

You, and hundreds of thousands of other Conservatives across this country. People who want inflation to go down, the out-of-control spending to end, the CBC to be defunded and all the hurt caused by Trudeau turned into hope for a better future.

*We can't count on the media to communicate our
messages to Canadians. We have to go around them
and their biased coverage. We need to do it directly
with ads, mail, phone calls and knocking on millions of
doors. And to do all that we need your help.*

Chip in to help us go around the biased media.

Thank you,

Pierre Poilievre

*PS. We can't take on the Liberals and the media and
win without your help.*

Chip in here: donate.conservative.ca

Of significance in this letter is that David Akin is accused of swearing, shouting, and heckling. Akin denies he was swearing. While he did interrupt Poilievre, it is a stretch to say he was shouting and heckling. The email suggests Akin's behaviour is an example of the media being "out to get" Poilievre and the Conservative Party. He says the party needs money to "go around the biased media." The PS makes it clear the Conservatives are not just fighting the other political parties; they are fighting the "Liberals and the media."

This is all part of creating a narrative. It is a story Conservative supporters believe; whether it's true or not is beside the point. The narrative takes on a life of its own.

This tactic is not new, but the threat to fair elections comes when there is no distinction made between opinion and fact. Reputable journalism is the only defence against the Wild West of unregulated social media platforms. It's not a surprise that Poilievre is pushing to defund the CBC and discredit the mainstream media.

He can't control the narrative with well-trained, disciplined journalists who are regulated by the Canadian Broadcast Council and laws related to libel and slander.

We've seen where this leads—it's right out of the Trump playbook. If politicians are worried they might lose an election, they tell their supporters their opponents are conspiring to rig the election so they will lose. The "Stop the Steal" narrative did not begin on election night in 2020 in the US. In fact, the slogan "Stop the Steal" has been a hallmark of nearly every election throughout Donald Trump's political career. It was first deployed in 2016 by Trump's long-time associate and confidant Roger Stone to defend Trump's Republican primary nomination, and later ramped up to contest Hillary Clinton's presidential bid.

And it didn't take long for supporters of Poilievre's style of politics to take to social media to spread the message to those who didn't get the fundraising letter. Clyde Do Something, a "current events commentator" on YouTube who has more than 140,000 subscribers, dissected the scrum video and said the media was accusing Pierre Poilievre of using "American-style politics" while they were using "American-style journalism tactics." He accused Akin of "grandstanding and trying to win the day as a reporter." Then he compared Akin to Jim Acosta, a CNN reporter who regularly questioned Donald Trump and the Trump administration. Trump famously called Acosta and the mainstream media "the enemy of the people." This was the narrative Clyde Do Something wanted to co-opt.

Acosta wrote a book about his time covering the Trump administration. In *The Enemy of the People: A Dangerous Time to Tell the Truth in America,* he says, "There must be a common understanding that words matter. They have meaning. Words have power. I believe the term 'the enemy of the people' will come to help define this era when one group of people was pitted against another in ways that I had not seen in my lifetime."

I agree with Acosta. Words matter—truth matters. I don't know who Clyde Do Something is when he is not stirring it up on YouTube; while he replied to my inquiries on Twitter, he did not provide his real name. He did ask me why I considered it dangerous to compare David Akin to Jim Acosta. My reply was that it's dangerous because it is a manipulation of the truth and a tactic used to rile up supporters.

All political parties create a narrative. Poilievre's Conservatives are not the first to do so. What has changed is the public's acceptance of the narratives that have a distinctly nasty tone.

In 1993, ten days before the federal election, the Progressive Conservatives launched an attack ad aimed at Jean Chrétien. It showed a very unflattering photo of his face and asked, "Is this a prime minister?" The ads had the tagline "Think twice."

The backlash was almost instantaneous. Chrétien has facial paralysis because of an illness he had as a child; the ads appeared to be making fun of that. After initially defending the ads, PC leader Kim Campbell announced they were being withdrawn. Even Conservative candidates declared the ads offensive and an act of desperation. The party's campaign manager, John Tory, didn't think anything was wrong with the ads, but he had to admit, "You can't argue with people when...they say they've taken offense." The Progressive Conservatives were trounced in the election ten days later, winning 2 seats to the Liberals' 177.

That ad may have backfired, but it was not the end of negative advertising. The parties quickly realized the key was to avoid basing their attacks on personal qualities. We have seen the Liberals, the Conservatives, and the NDP all use attack ads to brand their opponents negatively. The Conservatives used this tactic effectively when they aimed a series of attack ads at Michael Ignatieff, who was the leader of the Liberal Party and leader of the Official Opposition from 2008 to 2011. Shortly after he was elected leader in 2009, the Conservative Party started running ads that said Ignatieff was "just visiting." The four ads in the series asked why Ignatieff returned to Canada after thirty-four years away; they failed to mention that he had been teaching at Oxford, Cambridge, and Harvard. The ads suggested he was arrogant, lacked commitment, was not loyal to Canada, and would ruin the economy. They all ended with the line, "He's not in it for you—he's in it for himself. Michael Ignatieff— just visiting."

Analysts agree that this type of negative ad is effective when it is based on a kernel of truth, and the ads did influence the election two years later. Stephen Harper's Conservatives won a majority, and the Liberals ended up third with only thirty-four seats, losing their role as Official Opposition.

In the 2015 election, the Conservatives ran a series of ads branding Justin Trudeau as "just not ready." One ad depicted a group of people ostensibly making a hiring decision, with Justin Trudeau's resumé in their hands. It had some memorable lines: "Being prime minister is not an entry-level job." They write "just not ready" on Trudeau's application, and the voiceover echoes, "Justin Trudeau— he's just not ready." In the final shot, one of the actors says, "Nice hair, though."

Polling done a few months after the ad began airing showed it was having an impact on voters as the election approached. This may have been the reason the Liberals decided to address the ad head-on. It was a bold move, because politicians are often advised to ignore negative advertising to avoid giving it too much attention. The Liberal ad shows a confident Trudeau with his shirt sleeves rolled up, walking toward the camera with the Parliament buildings in the background. Trudeau says, "Stephen Harper says I'm not ready...I'm not ready to let this country fall into recession" and ends with "I'm ready to bring real change to Ottawa." Trudeau came across as strong and the ad took the wind out of the sails of the Tory ads.

In an odd twist, just a week after Pierre Poilievre was elected leader and began his attack on the media, the NDP began running a series of attack ads aimed at Poilievre. They used the line: "He's not in it for you" to counter Poilievre's populism and positioning as the anti-elite, working person's champion—traditionally the NDP's territory.

Democracy demands that we find ways to keep political narratives rooted in truth. When parties create untrue, deceptive, or destructive narratives, there should be consequences. We need to consider whether the current rules through the Elections Act ensure that citizens feel voting is free, fair, and meaningful. If not, we need to change those rules.

VOTING REVOLUTION TIP

Advocate for Canada to impose consequences, enforced through the Elections Act, when parties create untrue, deceptive, or destructive campaign narratives.

When it comes to controlling the narrative, here's a lesson from my own experience: if you are a candidate, it's essential that you define yourself. Do not make the mistake of leaving a gap for your opponents to fill in.

I was very new to politics when I became a Green Party candidate in 2015. I had covered politics for decades but had never been "inside" the political machine. Many people in Victoria knew me from my ten years as the CBC's afternoon-show host. I had also volunteered my time for hundreds of charities and was running as a Green candidate, so I thought it should have been obvious who I was and what I stood for. It seemed boastful to tell people how many degrees I had or all the awards I had won. As a young girl raised in the 1960s, I had been taught not to brag. Humility was considered a strength. (This is a trait that, in my experience, is more common in women than men.) Suddenly, I was expected to sell myself—to tell everyone I was better than my opponents. This was not my strong suit. (Ten-year-old Jo-Ann, who struggled a bit with humility, would have been a whiz at it, though.)

I knocked on doors and met voters with quiet confidence, sure that people would see I would be a good MP. At my first debate, I was surprised to hear the incumbent talk about himself and all the wonderful things he had done. He barely touched on the topics at hand. I had planned to leave all the stuff about me for my closing remarks, but guess what? We ran out of time, and they cut the closing remarks! Lesson learned.

So just as I was beginning to figure out that I should start talking about myself more—my political science degree, my awards—my volunteers told me that my opponents were referring to me as "the celebrity radio host," and they did not mean it in a good way. This was the time of the Jian Ghomeshi sexual assault scandal, and the term "celebrity radio host" implied someone who sounded good on the radio but wasn't necessarily who they appeared.

After that, I spent a lot of time correcting the narrative. I'll never know what role it played in my loss during that campaign. These days, I tell any candidate who wants advice that they must believe they are the best person for the job, and they should be prepared to tell voters why—often. Don't tear down opponents, just build your brand and sell it.

———

Here in Canada, a person doesn't run for "prime minister." The leader of the party that wins the majority of seats in an election is appointed prime minister by the governor general of Canada, who represents the monarchy. If there is no majority, then the governor general will ask the leader of the party with the most seats to see if they can pass a motion indicating that their party has the confidence of the House of Commons. In other words, enough MPs from other parties must support the leading party's motion to govern and agree with its proposed agenda. If that party loses a confidence vote, then the governor general can ask another party to see if it has the confidence of the House of Commons. This means the prime minister can be changed in Canada without an election.

Pierre Poilievre knows all this. He's been a member of Parliament since 2004, but you wouldn't know from listening to him. The day he announced he was running for the leadership of the

Conservative Party, Pierre Poilievre announced he was running for prime minister. In his launch video, he sits in front of a bookcase with pictures of his family and an interesting variety of books— George Orwell's *1984*; a biography of Julius Caesar; a biography of Ronald Reagan. He begins, "Governments have gotten big and bossy..." (Ironic, given that, as an MP, he is part of the government of Canada.) He lists the sins of the current Liberal government. Then he says, "That's why I'm running for prime minister—to put you back in charge of your life.... In a free country, smaller government makes room for bigger citizens."

This was his narrative: he was running for prime minister, even before he had won the Conservative leadership campaign. Even Conservative members who disagreed with the policies being put forward by Poilievre fell under the sway of the narrative. He made it clear he was the right choice for anyone who wanted a winner whose primary goal was to defeat Justin Trudeau. His message was that nothing else mattered—and it worked, because he won the leadership on the first ballot by a significant majority: 68 percent of the vote. Jean Charest came a distant second, with 16 percent of the vote.

This narrative means the next election will be about leaders, not individual candidates. Voters are being told that if they want Poilievre to be prime minister, they must vote Conservative, and it doesn't matter who their local candidate is.

This "cult of personality" approach isn't new. National advertising campaigns have been built around party leaders. It's the party leaders who face off in the televised debates after all, but the local MP still matters to voters. But this tactic—to make every vote cast for the party a vote for the leader—is a power play that's difficult to combat.

I do think there is a solution, though: take party affiliation off the ballot.

Having a political party's name listed on the ballot alongside the candidate's name is a relatively recent innovation. Political parties are not mentioned in the Canadian Constitution, the 1867 British North America Act, or in our 1982 Constitution Act. Political parties were not recognized in law until 1970 when the Canadian Elections Act was amended to include a process by which political parties could register and receive recognition.

This meant a party could place its name under the name of its candidate on the ballot, which happened for the first time in 1974. The change to the Elections Act also meant election spending could be more closely controlled. Both of these changes in legislation had an impact on our elections, but has that impact been positive? I don't think it has.

As it currently stands, all a voter must do to favour a particular party leader is to vote for the local candidate who has that party listed after their name on the ballot. The voter doesn't have to know anything about that candidate. In fact, in some cases, the parties would rather voters don't get to know much about their candidates at all. In the 2015, 2019, and 2021 elections, the Conservatives made a campaign decision not to attend local all-candidate debates in many ridings. The first time I showed up for a debate and was told the Conservative wouldn't be attending, I was shocked.

It was 2015 in Victoria, and we were at the Metropolitan United Church, a grand, classic building. The raised dais had been cleared of the altar and pulpit. In their place stood a long table with chairs and microphones for four candidates. The organizers had decided to make a point that the Conservative candidate wasn't coming, so they put a tie on a giant teddy bear and plunked him in the seat designated for the Conservative candidate. The nameplate in front of the bear bore the candidate's name: John Rizzuti. The church, with a seating capacity of six hundred people, was packed that night.

When Rizzuti was later asked why he hadn't attended the debate, he said he thought his time would be better spent knocking on doors—but there's no way Rizzuti reached six hundred people by knocking on doors that night. When the electoral votes were counted, Rizzuti had received 8,480 votes—almost 12 percent of the votes cast. I'm sure some of those votes were from friends and family, but most were essentially for Conservative leader Stephen Harper, even though his name wasn't on the ballot.

Taking the parties' names off the ballots might encourage voters to do their homework to find out more about who is running. A riding is much like a small town where the candidate is accountable to the voters. I believe removing the party name from the ballot would mean a return to political stories rooted in ridings—stories about a candidate people know because they see them at the market on Saturdays, or because the candidate helped out at the school variety show. If voters know something about the person they are electing, they are more likely to vote based on their values and to elect someone they can trust. This would mean voters would have a greater chance of feeling good about their vote.

VOTING REVOLUTION TIP

Encourage Elections Canada to experiment with taking the political party name off the ballot to encourage voters to elect a specific candidate rather than to blindly vote for a party. This would make local candidates more accountable to constituents during a campaign.

CHAPTER 7

MONEY MATTERS

All Campaigns Are Not Created Equal

ON DECEMBER 13, 1979, I WAS A KEEN YOUNG CBC RADIO reporter in Saint John, NB. That afternoon's newscasts had suggested Prime Minister Joe Clark's Progressive Conservative government might be defeated on a confidence vote on the budget that night.

I asked my news editor if he would approve the overtime if I came back to cover the story if it happened.

"It won't happen," he said. "It's sabre-rattling. But call me if you decide to come back."

I was twenty-three years old, single, and living alone in a small garret apartment in a century-old home. As the evening drew on, I got into my cozy nightgown. Snow began to fall as I paced the kitchen, listening for the votes as they were counted live on the parliamentary channel. When I heard that the Social Credit Party members had abstained, I knew the government would lose. I grabbed the phone and called my news editor as the final votes were counted.

"The government is falling, the government is falling," I cried into the phone, sounding a lot like Chicken Little. "Can I go into the office?"

"Sure," said my editor, who I'm sure was thinking, "This girl needs a life."

I changed and jumped into my coat, hat, and boots and grabbed my car keys. It was -8°C but I didn't care; this was one for the history books.

That night, I called every member of Parliament in New Brunswick to get their reactions—six Liberals, including Roméo LeBlanc (who would later become governor general), and four Progressive Conservatives. I fell asleep on the sofa at the station around 2:30 A.M., tired but satisfied that we had the best coverage of the government's defeat of any news outlet in the country. Even my boss, John Miller, was impressed and gave me kudos at the news meeting the next morning.

Joe Clark, then leader of the Progressive Conservative Party, on the boardwalk in Toronto's Beaches riding during the 1979 federal election campaign. [CANADA JACK, AKA JEREMY GILBERT, CC BY-SA 3.0, VIA WIKIMEDIA COMMONS]

Clark's defeat on a non-confidence motion by a vote of 139–133 came about because of his poor planning and because he had underestimated the opposition. He had a minority government. His party knew any bill that involved money would be a confidence vote. (The bill included raising the tax on gasoline by eighteen cents.) The PCs thought the bill would squeak through, but three Conservative MPs happened to be away. When the six Social Credit MPs who had previously supported the Conservative government said they wouldn't support this tax hike and announced they would abstain, the government fell, and an election was called for February 18, 1980.

The Liberals, led again by Pierre Trudeau, won a majority.

———

Nineteen years later, in November 2008, another minority Conservative government faced a non-confidence vote just six weeks after it had been elected. The issue, again, was money—in this case, the government's fiscal update, which contained plans to cut government spending. This time, the outcome was very different.

Here's how it went down.

In the fall of 2008, the Conservatives, led by Stephen Harper, formed their second minority government. The first one had lasted only two years and was criticized for having a nasty tone rather than one of cooperation, which is often the hallmark of a minority Parliament. Any existing goodwill toward the government evaporated when the opposition parties saw the Harper government's mini budget on November 27, 2008. It included a key proposal to eliminate the per-vote subsidy—the payment each political party received from the federal government to reflect its share of the popular vote in the previous election.

The Conservatives had not disclosed their plan to eliminate this political funding in their platform, so this move surprised the opposition parties. Harper knew this would upset them, but he was gambling that the parties wanted to avoid another election. The Conservatives thought the budget might be passed if they acted quickly. As it turned out, they figured wrong.

This move threatened to bankrupt the opposition parties. To understand why, we need to look at election financing in Canada.

In 1974, the Election Expenses Act was introduced. It put limits on election expenses for candidates and political parties. It also introduced public funding through partial reimbursements of election expenses, and tax credits for political contributions. The legislation was expanded in 2004 to include credits for local spending by political parties. Costs incurred in holding a contest to nominate a candidate were included, as was the cost of running for the leadership of a political party.

In 2003, the Liberal government introduced the per-vote subsidy, which paid qualifying political parties $1.75 per vote per year for every vote they had received in the previous election. This was part of a set of amendments designed to limit political contributions by individuals, corporations, unions, and non-profit groups. The theory was that with these limits—paired with the vote subsidy—political parties would rely less on unions, corporations, and wealthy donors and put greater importance on individual voters. Chrétien wanted to reduce the political influence of the rich and powerful and to recognize that, despite our first-past-the-post election system, every vote had some value. It was an attempt to correct the power imbalance in Canadian politics.

This made a big difference to smaller, emerging parties. It takes money to raise money, and when a party is not in power and doesn't have favours to bestow on donors, it is a challenge to raise funds on moral persuasion alone. It also helps address the voter question of, "If you aren't going to win, why would I vote for you?" I can say from experience that when a candidate knocks on a door and tells someone that, if they vote for them, their vote will help fund the party's work—even if they are not elected—it makes a difference. But most voters have never heard of the per-vote subsidy, and helping them understand why it matters is a challenge in a few minutes on a doorstep. And although it is less effective than providing proportional representation, it allows political parties to continue to balance the influence of corporations and wealthy lobbyists on government.

This was the subsidy Stephen Harper was hoping to eliminate. Philosophically, Harper and his Conservatives believed everything should be left to the free market. On principle, he wanted to reduce the role of government in the operation of political parties. Cutting taxpayers' funding of political parties was very on-brand for the former leader of the Canadian Alliance. On a practical level, he knew how vital the per-vote subsidy was to the health of the opposition parties—less so to his own.

Stephen Harper, former prime minister of Canada.
[REMY STEINEGGER, CC BY-SA 2.0, VIA WIKIMEDIA COMMONS]

Every party raises funds from supporters at both the party level and the riding level. The Conservatives raised $23.3 million to pay for the 2008 campaign, the Liberals $13.8 million, the NDP $5.05 million, the Bloc $1.43 million, and the Greens $1.45 million.

In terms of spending, according to Registered Party Returns on the Elections Canada website, the Conservative Party spent $19.5 million, the Liberals $14.6 million, the NDP $16.8 million, the Bloc $4.9 million, and the Greens $2.8 million. At that point, every party but the Conservatives would have been in a deficit position.

In addition to the per-vote subsidy, if a party gets more than 2 percent of the popular vote, it is eligible for a 50–60 percent rebate on election expenses. The parties rely on this rebate to repay their debt from expenses, and on the per-vote subsidy to offset the annual operating costs of running the party.

The Conservatives would have been in good shape after they received their rebate of $11.3 million, leaving them with $15.1 million, even without the per-vote subsidy of $10.4 million they received from that election. The Liberals would also have had a post-rebate ($7.54 million) surplus of $6.74 million; the per-vote subsidy then added $7.2 million to their coffers. The NDP, with a rebate of $3.62 million, still would have had a deficit of $8.13 million; the $5 million per-vote subsidy would still not lift them out of debt. The Bloc Québécois would have received a rebate of $2.46 million, with a remaining debt of $1.01 million which was then topped up by the per-vote subsidy of $2.7 million, leaving them in the black. The Greens would have still been in debt after their $0.5 million dollar rebate, facing a $0.85 million shortfall after the rebate, but the $1.9 million in per-vote subsidy would have left them on the positive side (see Table 1, page 133).

It's not hard to see how, of all the parties, the Conservatives needed the per-vote subsidy the least. This was not exactly a hidden agenda. In a *Globe and Mail* column in August 2008, Conservative strategist Tom Flanagan compared the Conservatives to "the rising Roman Republic" and the Liberals to "the evil empire of Carthage" in the third Punic War. In that fight, the Romans defeated Carthage, burned down the city, and sowed salt in the fields so nothing would grow again. Flanagan continued his comparison. "Destruction of the Liberals is not at hand...[but] they could be pushed into a financial pit they can never climb out of."

Harper had his opponents in his sights; it was not surprising they fought back. Within hours of introducing the economic update, it was clear the opposition members were determined

Table 1: Federal Election Funding, in $millions

Party	Funds raised	Election spending	Balance before rebate	Election expenses rebate	Balance after rebate	Per-vote subsidy	Final balance
Conservative Party	$23.30	$19.5	$3.80	$11.30	$15.10	$10.40	$25.50
Liberal Party	$13.80	$14.6	-$0.8	$7.54	$6.74	$7.20	$13.94
NDP	$5.05	$16.8	-$11.75	$3.62	-$8.13	$5.00	-$3.13
Bloc Québécois	$1.43	$4.9	-$3.47	$2.46	-$1.01	$2.70	$1.69
Green Party	$1.45	$2.8	-$1.35	$0.50	-$0.85	$1.90	$1.05

Sources: Elections Canada: Registered Party Returns in Respect of General Election Expenses
Elections Canada: Past Elections > 40th General Election, October 14, 2008

to vote non-confidence. A confidence vote was scheduled for December 1 but was delayed by a week. The Liberals and the NDP put aside their differences in an agreement that would create a coalition government with a commitment from the Bloc Québécois to avoid non-confidence motions on an agreed list of subjects.

The battle lines were drawn. The Conservative communications teams set about to paint this coalition arrangement as something nefarious. Conservative MPs and many in the media started referring to this as a "constitutional crisis." Both sides were now describing the situation as a crisis when, in fact, Canada's democratic principles allowed for such a scenario. If the government lost a confidence vote, the governor general could allow the Liberal–NDP coalition a chance to govern or to call an election. The prime minister didn't want either outcome. He referred to the coalition as an anti-democratic power grab and a "separatist coalition" because it included the Bloc. This language raised the issue of national unity, and anger was mounting.

The Conservatives had a plan. They would get Parliament shut down so that the vote could not be held. Elizabeth May, the leader of the Green Party of Canada then (but not an elected MP), later wrote a detailed account of these events in her book *Losing Confidence: Power, Politics and the Crisis in Canadian Democracy.* "Never in the history of modern parliamentary democracies anywhere in the world had a prime minister sought to close down the government to avoid losing a confidence vote," she wrote.

The governor general, Michaëlle Jean, allowed the prorogation of Parliament two weeks after it had opened. It was, and remains to this day, a dangerous precedent and an ugly moment in Canadian history. Nelson Wiseman, a professor of political science at the University of Toronto, told the *New York Times,* "This really has been a blow to parliamentary democracy in Canada. It has lowered the status of the elected Parliament and raised the status of the unelected prime minister." Ronald Wright, in his book *A Short History of Progress,* criticized the actions of the Harper government, noting that modern parliamentary democracy rests on a single great principle: "The government must have the consent of the governed. The people delegate this consent to their MPs.... When the government cannot carry the House, it falls." He concluded that, given "the precedent of Harper's coup d'*état*...any future government can now slip the leash of democracy similarly. This is how constitutions fail."

When Parliament resumed, the government withdrew its plan to remove the per-vote subsidy. The Harper government no longer faced a non-confidence vote, and the financial ruin of the opposition parties was avoided. A battle had been won, but the war on the public financing of political parties was far from over.

The reprieve did not last long. In the 2011 election, Stephen Harper's Conservatives won a majority government and soon announced that, beginning in 2012, the federal per-vote subsidy would be phased out.

This time, the move succeeded. The subsidy was gone by 2015. What remains in its place are tax credits for anyone who donates to a political party—so political parties now run never-ending fundraising campaigns. There are still limits on donations by corporations, unions, and individuals, but the loss of the subsidy has shifted the power dynamic in Canadian politics. With the per-vote subsidy, every voter could make a difference to their chosen party through an indirect contribution. Now political parties receive public funding only from people who have disposable income—and who can afford to donate directly.

And this is the problem: very few Canadians directly support Canadian democratic institutions financially, and those who do tend to be in higher income brackets. In 2013, 7 percent of people aged twenty-five to sixty-four whose personal income was $80,000 or more were members or participants in a political party or group; this was the case for just 3 percent of those whose personal income was under $40,000.

A party that depends on appeals to those who earn enough to want a significant tax break is more likely to have policies that appeal to economically advantaged people. If a party hopes CEOs and corporate board members will donate, it is more likely to create legislation they like. The same is true with special interest groups.

The "Freedom Convoy" raised millions of dollars in donations by appealing to thousands of people who felt disenfranchised. To tap into an emotional response like that, it's necessary to create an "us versus them" mentality that is not good for society in the long run.

So a relatively small number of Canadians is determining, through their donations, where the federal funding for political parties goes. The majority of Canadians no longer have any influence on which parties their own tax money funds. The per-vote subsidy was a much more democratic way of financing political parties.

This change in party funding indirectly feeds voter cynicism. When Elections Canada surveyed non-voters about why they didn't vote, the most common answer was, "Because my vote doesn't matter."

VOTING REVOLUTION TIP

Persuade government to bring back the per-vote subsidy. This is the single most significant change we can make to election financing and the simplest way, barring proportional representation, to make every vote matter and let the public know their vote has value.

Running for office is an expensive proposition, and not just for the parties themselves. It is often hard for political parties to find candidates who are willing to run because there are very few professions where a person can take several weeks off work with no salary to apply for a job they may not get. But that is precisely what we ask candidates to do in an election.

This explains why the makeup of Parliament does not reflect our population. In 2021, Parliament had a record number of women—104—but this was still just 30.7 percent of MPs, despite the best efforts of several groups dedicated to attaining gender parity in the House of Commons. Also in 2021, the highest number ever of people of colour was elected to Parliament, with 53 MPs (15.7 percent of the House of Commons). The average age of MPs is fifty-two, and there are more lawyers than any other profession; farmers are second and business people are third.

When I ran in Victoria, BC, in 2015, I had a well-funded campaign. I was in a riding the party hoped to win, and the party was willing to provide funds to help support me as a candidate. We spent $148,000. We did have some paid positions, but we couldn't have managed the campaign without the more than two hundred active volunteers we had; they were the heart and soul of that campaign. I received a modest stipend every month. It made all the difference to me; I couldn't have managed without it.

I have always been haunted by the money spent by my opponent who won the riding in 2015. Murray Rankin, the New Democrat who was the incumbent, spent $222,000. He was fifth among the candidates in Canada with the highest spending. I often joke that it took a lot of money to beat me.

When I ran in Halifax in 2019, it was a different story. Every penny we raised had to be spent on the campaign. There was no money to help support the candidate. Luckily, I had a small pension and had reduced my living expenses when we moved from Victoria to Halifax. I was also Deputy Leader of the Green Party of Canada, which provided me with a part-time salary. In the end, I spent $46,000 and the winner spent $77,000. The person who came second spent $92,000—so spending more money is not always the answer.

Our daughter Claire also ran in the 2019 election. I'm admittedly biased, but Claire is everything a voter wants in a candidate. She is bilingual, has a master's degree in immigration and settlement, and is a registered immigration consultant. She is in her mid-thirties, loves people, and is passionate about social justice, climate action, and making the world better.

But when she called to get my opinion on whether she should run, I was hesitant. I knew I would be busy running my own campaign, so I wouldn't be able offer her much help. She was running against a well-established Liberal cabinet minister. It would be a tough race. As a mother, I worried about how hard it would be for her financially. She would have to take a leave of absence from her job. She lived simply, with no car and reasonable rent, but she did have a student loan she was trying to pay off.

Ultimately, she put her name forward and won the contested nomination. She ran an outstanding campaign, finishing third with 18 percent of the vote—an increase of 13 percent over the Green Party's vote in the previous election. Her campaign spent $19,000. When it was over, Claire returned to her job and started catching up on the personal expenses she had built up while campaigning. She loved the experience, and I hope she will do it again; the country needs people like Claire to be involved. However, when she was asked to run again in the same riding in 2021, she said no. She couldn't afford to. She had bought a house and a car and had just been married; her husband wasn't working. She had a new job and was running her own immigration consulting business.

To run, she would have needed some form of income during the campaign.

Claire is not alone. In every election, hundreds of potential candidates decide they can't run because they can't afford it. That means we are more likely to elect MPs who have had well-paid jobs or jobs where having a high political profile with a party that might form government is good for their career. Many businesses don't want to be associated with any party platform and aren't willing to give their employees time off to run in an election.

What if we could find a way to show we value political involvement? I propose we introduce a political candidate allowance. To be eligible, a candidate would have to win the nomination of a registered political party in a valid electoral district. Once they had won the nomination, they could apply for the political candidate allowance. This monthly income-replacement allowance, which could be used if a person took a leave without pay from a salaried job, could be claimed for at least one month and up to twelve months during an election year. It would be based on the living wage for the riding, and paid monthly.

This would make becoming a candidate accessible to a wider range of people and encourage more diversity in the political process. As Canadians, we value a variety of voices and opinions in our democracy. If we want more diversity in our elected officials, we must eliminate barriers to running for office. It is time for

VOTING REVOLUTION TIP

Have government introduce a monthly income-replacement allowance for political candidates. This would level the playing field and make becoming a candidate accessible to a more diverse range of people.

Canadians to value running for office and see it as a contribution to our society that is worthy of compensation.

Again, it would signal that we, as a society, consider political activity valuable and essential in our democracy; it would help level the playing field. This is how we can use money for good—our common good.

CHAPTER 8

UNFAIR ADVANTAGE

The Myth of Fixed Election Dates

'VE KNOWN DAVID COON, THE LEADER OF THE GREEN Party of NB, for a long time. When I was the host of CBC Radio's *Information Morning* in Moncton, and he was with the Conservation Council of New Brunswick I interviewed him about environmental issues. I have always admired his knowledge, his commitment to his values, and his integrity. We worked together on a few Green Party events when I left journalism and moved to politics.

His wife, Janice Harvey, also has a brilliant political mind, and she and I have spent many enjoyable evenings solving the world's problems over a glass of wine. Despite this history and growing friendship, I had never worked directly for Coon, so I was surprised when I received a call from him in September 2023.

"Hey Jo-Ann," he said, "I want you to be our campaign manager for the next provincial election. Will you do it?"

I gave him a few reasons why I wasn't sure I was the right person for the job but, in the end, I accepted. Aside from being surprised Coon wanted me for the job, I was also surprised by the timing of the request because, technically, the next provincial election in New Brunswick was a year away. It was unusual for the NB Greens to hire a campaign manager a year ahead; they didn't have the budget to have a full-time campaign manager for a year.

"Why now?" I asked.

"[Premier] Blaine Higgs is giving every indication he will call a snap election," he said. "We have to be ready." Indeed, there were some substantial clues that the premier was planning to go to the polls. He had rented a bus and wrapped it in PC colours, complete with his larger-than-life smiling face. Elections New Brunswick was renting voting locations and training staff in preparation for an early vote.

New Brunswick Green Party leader David Coon and Jo-Ann Roberts at the Seaport Market in Halifax, NS, December 4, 2022. [KEN KELLY]

I packed a bag and moved to Fredericton for most of the month of October. Over the next few weeks, I thought of nothing else but what needed to be done to get ready to go to the polls a year ahead of schedule. We recruited candidates, fast-tracked vetting and nomination meetings, designed signs and brochures, and worked on a platform. Our office buzzed with rumours and speculation: "Will he or won't he?"

In the end, he didn't; Premier Higgs changed his mind. But it was an expensive exercise. A few months later, Kim

Poffenroth, New Brunswick's Chief Electoral Officer, explained to a legislature committee that Elections New Brunswick had no choice but to be ready, given the statements by the premier. Poffenroth reported that Elections NB had spent $1,750,808 on polling station rentals, returning office rentals, phone and internet connections, and the training of returning officers.

The fact that the election didn't happen was perhaps just as well for the Greens. We had scrambled to find candidates when we thought we might go into a snap election. Many interested people couldn't commit on short notice. The party would have had a full slate, but more than half of them would have been "paper candidates" whose names were on the ballot but who would have been unable to run a full campaign. In the end, by holding off until the fixed date in October 2024, the NB Greens ran close to a full slate—forty-six out of forty-nine candidates, with many of them actively running campaigns. The party went from three seats to two and lost 1.5 percent of its popular vote, but David Coon handily won his own riding.

There is much speculation as to why Blaine Higgs decided not to go to the polls early. He faced division within his caucus and likely wanted to eliminate some troublemakers, but in truth he wasn't doing well in the polls. Some federal Conservative heavyweights were seen in Fredericton around that time, and it is believed they convinced him that going to the polls early was a risk he shouldn't take. In the end, Higgs would lose his seat in the October 2024 election anyway, and his party would be defeated; the Liberals won a majority government, with Susan Holt becoming the province's first female premier.

But Higgs's near–election call is a great example of the problem with Canada's current fixed–election date legislation: nothing can stop a premier or a prime minister from ignoring the fixed date and calling an early vote. If they think they can make it work for them, then why not? Higgs had done it before.

Ignoring a fixed election date also sends the wrong message to voters. Calling an early election for no apparent reason signals to voters that it's right for politicians to ignore the rules if it they think it will keep them in power. No wonder voters are cynical.

We often refer to elections as horse races. In racing, there's an understanding that a good start is half the battle. But what if one of the jockeys could just decide when to start the race? Only that person would know when it would happen, and they could sound the bell and open the gate while the other jockeys were still warming up.

There's no way anyone would think that was fair. As for the spectators and those placing bets, eventually only the few who were friends with the jockey in control of the start would bother turning up. The rest would walk away, knowing the race was fixed.

Knowing when an election will be called gives the party in power a distinct advantage. Premiers and prime ministers have ignored fixed-election legislation left and right since it was first introduced in Canada in 2007 by Prime Minister Stephen Harper.

"Fixed election dates prevent governments from calling snap elections for short-term political advantage," Harper said then. "They level the playing field for all parties, and the rules are clear for everybody."

That sounds good, but there is a loophole big enough to drive a campaign bus through. The federal act says, "Nothing in this section affects the power of the governor general, including the power to dissolve Parliament at the governor general's discretion." In other words, if a leader asks for an election, they get an election. There are no criteria for when a leader can ignore the fixed date and there is no penalty for jumping the gun.

The ink was barely dry on the new federal fixed–election date legislation when Stephen Harper himself decided to break it and go to the polls in 2008 instead of 2009. Democracy Watch, a national non-partisan citizen group advocating democratic reform and government accountability, challenged the government in court. They lost. The judge ruled, "The remedy for the applicant's contention is not for the federal court to decide but rather one of the count of the ballot box." In other words, it's up to voters to punish a party that breaks its promise.

Well, the voters didn't get the memo in 2008. They didn't punish Harper; they rewarded him by increasing his number of seats in the House by sixteen.

In September 2021, Prime Minister Justin Trudeau thought this tactic would work for him a well. He called an election two years ahead of the fixed election date. The election cost $630 million, and when it was over almost nothing had changed—Trudeau still had a minority government.

The provinces and territories in Canada also have fixed–election date legislation that tends to be ignored. In New Brunswick in 2020, during the COVID-19 pandemic, Premier Blaine Higgs called a snap election two years into his minority government. His gamble paid off: he won a majority.

A month later, across the country in British Columbia, John Horgan was also leading a minority government. He called a snap election, and he also won a majority.

Then there's Dennis King. In March 2023, the Progressive Conservative premier of PEI bet that he could ignore the fixed election date in his province and not be punished at the polls. The election was held on April 3 and King won a huge majority. There would be no more minority government in which he had to work with the Greens, who were then the Official Opposition. King went from thirteen to twenty-two seats, and the Greens dropped from eight to two seats. However, Canadian democracy paid a price. The voter turnout in the PEI election dropped to its lowest level ever (68.5 percent of registered voters), and that's no accident. Premier King called an election when he knew he could win, and the voters got the message. They figured it out: if the outcome is a slam dunk, why bother voting? (This, in a province that has consistently had one of the best voter turnouts in the country.)

What's interesting is that the PEI election took place only six months ahead of the fixed date. When he was asked why he was calling the election in March instead of October, Premier King just said, "It's four years; it's time to have an election." King added that there was a chance of a federal election later that year, given that Prime Minister Justin Trudeau was leading a minority government. "There's uncertainty in Ottawa," he said. "There could be a fall election. Part of the reason our election was moved [is] because of the election dates in Ottawa."

I hate to be cynical, but despite what he says, I don't think that's the whole reason King called the election six months ahead of schedule. There were likely a couple of other reasons. First, he wanted to capitalize on PEI's successful hosting of the Canada Winter Games. Islanders were proud of themselves and gave the government credit for making a good impression on the national stage. Second, the other parties weren't ready. They thought they were working toward a fall election, and the snap election call caught them off guard. The PCs were the only party to have all twenty-seven candidates nominated and ready to campaign the day King called the vote.

Dennis King was going to the polls early because he knew he could win. Voters believed him and figured there was no great urgency to vote; the outcome was a foregone conclusion.

Democracy Watch has launched court proceedings challenging the rights of premiers and prime ministers to call snap elections.

***

Snap elections are not good for democracy; they are particularly unfair to opposition parties, which don't have as many resources as the party in power. Those parties have fewer elected members than the governing party, and that makes a difference leading up to an election. MLAs and MPs have regular contact with the voters. If they are good at their jobs, they are well known in their ridings; they send out regular newsletters telling voters what they are doing, and they are often invited to attend high-profile events. It is the advantage of being the incumbent.

But for those seeking to oppose an incumbent MLA or MP, it's best to start early—months before an election. This obviously isn't possible with a snap election. It's also harder for opposition parties to recruit candidates, since not everyone can put their life on hold for a month at a moment's notice; this is particularly true for women. With a fixed election date, a potential candidate can plan to take vacation days or apply for a leave of absence from their job to allow them to be actively involved in campaigning.

I've felt the impact of a snap election call personally; when I was approached to run for the first time, I thought I knew when the election was going to be held. It never occurred to me there might be a snap election. I weighed the pros and cons of putting my name on the ballot, and it helped that I thought I had at least eight or nine months to prepare. I knew I would need time to build a team, raise money, and get out and meet voters. I also had to manage my personal life; our son and daughter-in-law were expecting our first grandchild, and we had planned a family trip to PEI to introduce our grandchild to our family members on the east coast.

Then Stephen Harper called the election a few weeks earlier than expected. My family and I were at our granddaughter's baptism in North Rustico, PEI, when Harper emerged from Rideau Hall and announced the election was under way. My family members finished their vacation, but I jumped on a plane to return to Victoria

Jo-Ann Roberts with family at Ross Lane Beach, Stanhope, PEI, August 2023. L–R: Eugenio Kelly-Orozco, Claire Kelly-Orozco, Paul Donaldson, Megan (Kelly) Donaldson, Lauren Bercovitch Kelly (holding Mae Kelly), Christopher Kelly, Pat LePoidevin, Aly Kelly (holding Miles Kelly), Georgia Kelly, Jo-Ann Roberts, and Ken Kelly. [Laura Green]

for what turned out to be the most protracted federal campaign—despite the fact that it had been a snap call—in Canadian history.

———

Nova Scotia was the last province in Canada to enshrine a fixed election date. It was one of the first things Premier Tim Houston did when he was elected premier of Nova Scotia in August 2021. The first fixed election date chosen was July 15, 2025, and subsequent elections were to be held on the third Tuesday in July every fourth calendar year thereafter.

In July! Summer elections in a province that thrives on tourism?

When the legislation was introduced, I, along with dozens of teachers and political scientists, appeared before the Law Amendments Committee to try to convince the government that, although having a fixed election date was a good idea, having it in July was not. In my brief, I pointed out to the committee that, of the sixty-four elections held in Nova Scotia since Confederation, only seven had been held in the summer. Tellingly, all three of the summer elections that had been held since 1999 had been won by Conservatives. It doesn't take a cynic to see the connection; with much of the province on holiday and much of the other half working in the tourism industry, voter turnout is guaranteed to drop—favouring the Conservatives, who have a loyal voter base in Nova Scotia.

Of course, that wasn't the reason Premier Houston gave for choosing a summer date. He was reported to have said: "The schools are vacant. We can use the schools to set up polling stations."

Feel free to roll your eyes. At least a dozen teachers appeared before the Law Amendments Committee to point out that it would harm the schools' ability to teach students about democracy if the elections were held during the summer when schools weren't in session. Teachers said they often use elections to teach civics. The government's response was that teachers could surely find other ways to teach civics and pointed out that more students would be available to volunteer on campaigns. Personally, I had spent a lot of time in schools during my two federal campaigns and had seen first-hand the immediate influence an election campaign has on students.

And guess what? In 2024, Houston did call a snap election and won a supermajority, with a voter turnout of just 45 percent—one of the lowest voter turnouts in Nova Scotia history.

"When it comes time for the people to have their say, I think it would be pretty selfish for me to say, 'No, you have to wait because it doesn't suit the provincial legislation that was passed,'" Houston was reported as saying in June 2024. "That's a good thing. It will bring predictability to our elections. And our elections, of course, are the cornerstone of our democracy."

And we wonder why voters lack trust in politicians. Nova Scotia NDP leader Claudia Chender, who became the official opposition leader in that election, told a reporter earlier: "When the premier decides to go to the polls will have nothing to do with when Nova Scotians should have a voice and everything to do with when he thinks he can win."

Before 2022, the United Kingdom had what I considered some of the best legislation regarding fixed election dates. Their rules stated, as our federal rules do, that a government could call an early election if it lost a vote of confidence in the House of Commons. But here's the biggest difference: a UK government could also decide to call an early election if a supermajority of MPs—meaning two-thirds of MPs in the House of Commons—agreed to an early vote. Using this requirement, if Dennis King had put his early election idea to a vote, it's unlikely the Liberals or the Greens would have supported the idea.

However, like their Canadian counterparts, British politicians didn't like having a restriction on when they could call an election. The Fixed-term Parliaments Act (FTPA) had been passed in 2011, but like many things in Britain, it became a political football during Brexit. In 2019, the Conservatives, under Theresa May, campaigned to repeal the act. They said the FTPA had "led to paralysis at a time when the country needed decisive action."

When May stepped down in 2019 and Boris Johnson became prime minister, he tried three times to call an election under FTPA by calling for a vote in the House of Commons. He failed to get the required two-thirds majority all three times. Frustrated, he decided to use his majority in the House of Commons to circumvent the FTPA. He introduced the Early Parliamentary General Election Act on October 29, calling for an election on December 12, 2019. It was fast-tracked through Parliament, given Royal Assent, and became law. Parliament was dissolved on November 6, and the country went to the polls.

Johnson won a huge majority, and the days were numbered for the FTPA, which was repealed in 2022. Making a request of the monarch became the only requirement for a government to call an early election before the five-year limit. The repeal legislation also added a section that made it clear that no court could question the exercise or purported exercise of those powers. The United Kingdom went from having the strongest legislation to having legislation that makes it easy for the party in power to call an election. When historians look back on this time, they might conclude that this is a case of a majority government rigging the system to give themselves the tools to stay in power as long as possible.

There are many aspects of US-style democracy that are not working right now, but I must admit I'm a little envious of that country's iron-clad fixed election dates. Short of a revolution, there is no way to change when Americans go to the polls. The criticism of this is that the Americans always seem to be in election mode. Much of that is due to the fact that mid-term elections are held two years after the presidential election, meaning Americans vote every two years.

However, having a fixed election date doesn't seem to make for exceptional voter turnout in the US. Americans rank thirty-first for voting-age population turnout among the fifty Organisation for Economic Co-operation and Development (OECD) countries. Still, it's better than Canada's turnout, which ranks forty-third.

There must be a happy medium between an absolute fixed election date and allowing the party in power to call an election whenever it feels it can win. As we've seen, policies like this do not serve democracy. They make the public cynical; voters give up because they know the system is not fair.

Here's my suggestion: Fixed election dates must be more than just glorified guidelines. There should be a required reason to call an early election that has the support of more than just the governing party. Alternatively, the governing party should be required to provide a specific amount of notice—sixty or ninety days—to call an early election. This would eliminate some of the unfair advantage for the party in power. It would also mean opposition parties could spend less time guessing about a possible election call.

If any of the court challenges by Democracy Watch succeed, the courts in Canada may end up directing Parliament to add some restraints to the fixed-election legislation. I hope they do. It's time to put some hobbles on these prancing ponies—premiers and prime ministers who think they have free rein to use their power to fix the race.

But in the meantime, if we don't want politicians to ignore fixed election dates, we shouldn't vote for them when they do.

VOTING REVOLUTION TIP

Advocate for fixed election dates that are truly fixed, with strict criteria for not adhering to them. Allow a governing party to adjust election dates only with a valid reason that is supported by other parties. Alternatively, require a specific amount of notice—sixty or ninety days—to call an early election.

CHAPTER 9

MANDATORY VOTING

The Australian Example

ANNA KEENAN IS PASSIONATE ABOUT DEMOCRACY. She has devoted much of her life to democratic action and has worked for climate action and electoral reform causes. She has been a Green Party candidate in two federal elections, running in her rural riding of Malpeque, PEI, and has served on the board of Fair Vote Canada. Keenan was born and raised in Brisbane, Australia, and later moved to Montréal, where she met the love of her life. Together they moved to a farm in his home province of PEI, where they now live with their son.

Keenan hasn't lived in Australia for more than a decade but retains a hint of her Aussie accent. Her Australian roots have influenced her opinion on the practice of mandatory voting, which she thinks would be a game-changer for Canada.

Voting wasn't always mandatory in Australia. It was voluntary for the first nine elections. However, when voter turnout in 1922 dropped to less than 60 percent from more than 71 percent in 1919, a private member's bill was passed, making it compulsory to cast a ballot—and it worked. Voter turnout jumped to over 91 percent in 1925. The turnout in Australian elections has never fallen below 90 percent since then.

People love voting day in Australia, Keenan says. "It's held on a Saturday, and the atmosphere is festive." She says voting often takes place at local schools, and parent committees from those schools use the occasion to hold fundraising barbecues.

"Everybody looks forward to the 'sausage sizzles,'" she says, "and they line up to get their 'democracy sausages.' It's a party. Everybody shows up, including the local political parties."

Keenan says when she first became a Canadian citizen and could vote here, she found it odd that there was no political presence around the polling stations. In Canada, no campaigning is allowed on election day, and candidates and their representatives, by law, need to keep anything that might influence the voter away from polling stations. In Australia, campaigning at polling stations is not only legal, but encouraged. Political parties set up tables outside the polling places and provide information on their policies and candidates.

"It gives people, especially those not paying attention, a chance to be better informed before they vote," says Keenan.

Keenan also found out what happens if you don't vote in Australia. She was travelling in Europe and couldn't get home for a state election; she also wasn't able to vote by mail. After the election, a letter arrived asking why she hadn't voted. It stated that if she had no legitimate reason for not voting, she would be fined fifty dollars as a first-time offender at the state level. The fine for not voting at the federal level is twenty dollars. Keenan wrote back, explaining that she had been out of the country on voting day. She was excused and the fine was waived.

———

When I mention that I am writing a book on getting more people to vote in Canada, many people immediately say, "We should have mandatory voting like they do in Australia." Australia seems to be the best-known place for mandatory voting, but more than twenty countries have such a law, although not all of them enforce it. And, while voting is compulsory in Australia, Australia isn't even in the top ten countries with the highest voter turnout—it's number twelve. Still, twelfth place is much better than Canada's forty-third place.

The terms "mandatory voting" and "compulsory voting" are actually slight misnomers. What is usually mandatory is attendance at the polls. A voter in many of these countries does not have to cast a ballot; all they have to do is show up at the polling station. Many countries allow a person to choose "none of the above," or to spoil their ballot or write "I do not wish to vote." This is a crucial democratic tenet that respects an individual's right to abstain from supporting any of the parties on the ballot.

I know from experience that when someone chooses "none of the above" instead of voting for a particular candidate, it sends a message. Green Party policy, federally and provincially, allows for "none of the above" in every internal election, even if only one candidate is running. In 2021, this scenario played out when I ran to become deputy leader of the Green Party of Nova Scotia. No one ran against me, so I was confident I would win, and I did. However, when the votes were counted, a handful of people—three or four— had chosen "none of the above." It was humbling, but it was a good a reminder that those members deserved to be heard. Their vote sent a message that I certainly took seriously. I did my best while in that office to ensure I listened to those who disagreed with me, as I did not have a universal mandate.

We don't see enough of this in Canadian politicians or political systems. Much of the frustration and anger expressed by Canadian voters is a result of feeling ignored. It's worth asking if there is value in adding a "none of the above" option to our ballots. Indeed, if compulsory voting were introduced in Canada, voters would want that choice.

Australia doesn't have a "none of the above" option, but there have been "spoil the ballot" campaigns to tell politicians that voters are unhappy with the vote. Putting a blank ballot in the box is one form of protest; another is to scribble another name on the ballot. In 2016, 5 percent of Australians spoiled their ballots, and the voter turnout was 94 percent. Compare that with the 2019 federal election in Canada, where the voter turnout was 67 percent and the number of rejected (spoiled) ballots was 1 percent. It's hard to know exactly how many of the 33 percent of Canadians who didn't vote in that election were simply sending a message and might have spoiled their ballot if there were mandatory voting. In Australia, they don't have to guess. They know that with a 94 percent turnout, 5 percent of those who voted were not happy with the choices.

In 2016, the ERRE—the House of Commons Special Committee on Electoral Reform—considered whether mandatory voting would be appropriate for Canada. The Australian Electoral Commissioner, Tom

Rogers, testified before the committee, noting that compulsory voting and enrolment are seen as a normal part of Australian political culture. He also explained that non-voters are sent a letter that requires them to provide a valid excuse or pay a small fine. He says a small number of those who don't pay the fine are then prosecuted. "I think we went through a full prosecution of about three thousand people at the last election," he said. That percentage is miniscule, given that 15.6 million people voted in that election.

When the ERRE travelled to Charlottetown for hearings, Anna Keenan made a presentation. The hearings were held at a waterfront hotel with grand views of Charlottetown Harbour—the body of water by which the Fathers of Confederation had arrived in 1864 to discuss forming the Dominion of Canada.

Keenan told the committee she was surprised to learn when she came to Canada that voting was optional. She said her support for mandatory voting is rooted in how it changes campaigning. "I had never heard of a 'Get Out the Vote' campaign before I left Australia," she told the committee. "Everybody is already going to come out and vote. The campaigning becomes a lot more about issues and policies."

Keenan makes a good point. Political parties spend a great deal of time and money on Get Out the Vote (GOTV) efforts. Every campaign manager in Canada knows that door-knocking wins elections; the primary goal is to introduce your candidate to voters, but in Canada there is another critical underlying goal. Political parties are trying to find out where their support is. They take the voters list, create walk sheets that map out the route for canvassers, and go door to door asking questions about issues and telling voters about their candidate. Canvassers also want to know if the person who answers the door is a supporter. If they are, it is the party's job to ensure they vote before they change their mind.

To be honest, this has been a weakness for the Green Party, both provincially and federally. It takes a lot of resources to run an effective GOTV campaign, and for a long time Greens thought it was more important to have a good platform and win debates than to simply identify their voters and get them out to the polls. Imagine if going to the polls was looked after, and political parties could go back to listening to voters' concerns, discussing issues, and focussing on why a particular candidate would be the best choice. From the point of view of levelling the playing field, mandatory voting makes a lot of sense.

So the first argument in favour of mandatory voting is that it eliminates the need for political parties to spend time and money on GOTV campaigns. This argument is unlikely to appeal to the Liberal or Conservative parties, however, as they stand to gain very little from it. They have invested in highly sophisticated technology to track voters and support. They have designed their campaigns to work with the current system. They know how to win using this system and these tools. They also have years of historical voting data and would not want to walk away from that.

The second argument in favour of mandatory voting is that having more people vote increases the strength of the mandate given to those who are elected. Let's take, for example, Premier Doug Ford's win in Ontario in 2022. The province recorded the lowest voter turnout in history during that election. Just 43.5 percent of eligible voters cast a ballot, and Ford's PCs won with only 40.8 percent of that vote—17.6 percent of eligible voters—and yet he won a majority government. It's hard to claim democratic legitimacy or a strong mandate based on those numbers, but it certainly hasn't reduced that government's powers.

The third argument in favour of mandatory voting is that it reduces the power inequity between those who turn out to vote and those who don't. Research shows that people with lower income and education levels are less likely to vote. Mandating citizens to vote changes the balance of who gets to have their say.

Elections Canada, in conjunction with academic researchers, produces data on voter demographics after every election. Historically, politicians and political operatives have been very conscious of who votes so they can cater their political platforms to them. In 2019, the federal Liberals promised to cut taxes for "the middle class and the people working hard to join it." Seniors and veterans are also strong voting blocks, so every major political party includes platform planks that speak directly to them.

If voting were mandatory, political parties would have to consider the interests of all voters, regardless of their socio-economic status, level of education, or ability to mobilize or motivate. This could change everything, but as Nelson Wiseman, professor of Political Science at the University of Toronto, told the committee, "I just don't think it's in the interests of most MPs to do it."

When the ERRE asked Canadians how they felt about compulsory voting in an online survey, 22,247 people responded. They were asked if they agreed or disagreed with the statement, "Canadians should be required to cast a ballot in a federal election (this could include spoiling a ballot)." Just over half of the

VOTING REVOLUTION TIP

Actively support mandatory voting because it eliminates the need for political parties to spend time and money on GOTV campaigns and because having more people vote increases the democratic legitimacy of the mandate given to those who are elected. It also reduces the power inequity between those who typically vote and those who don't.

respondents supported the idea of compulsory voting: 36.2 percent strongly agreed and 14.1 percent agreed (totalling 50.3 percent), while 8.3 percent disagreed and 28.0 percent strongly disagreed (adding up to 36.3 percent). Almost 10 percent were undecided.

***

Despite the many arguments in support of mandatory voting, in the end, the ERRE recommended against implementing it. They agreed it would change campaigning, make voting more equal by ensuring input from those who traditionally do not vote, and address the problem of declining voter turnout.

"However," the report said,

> ...some members of the Committee also appreciated the argument that the right to vote includes the right not to vote, or even to present oneself at the polls, and that the decision to do so should be made freely. As well, the Committee recognizes that introducing mandatory voting would not in itself resolve the root causes of low voter turnout or engagement and might mask them. Finally, the Committee acknowledges the general discomfort expressed with penalizing people for not participating in the electoral process, particularly those with a disability.

Some who oppose mandatory voting argue that voting is a right that inherently includes the option to not exercise it. The argument is that if citizens are free to vote they have to also be free to not vote.

Don Desserud, a professor of political science at the University of Prince Edward Island, made this argument in his presentation to the committee: "My concern is that we're missing the point," he said. "Yes, voting is a civic duty and is itself a form of civic engagement, but it is also a measure, a reflection of the engagement of the community. In other words, people are not voting for other reasons than simply because they haven't been nudged, and if we have mandatory voting, we risk overlooking those or masking those."

Elections Canada has studied why people don't vote and concluded that making voting easier and more accessible would help, but that these are not the primary reasons people, especially young people, don't vote. A primary reason is lack of motivation. Abstainers don't think their vote will make a difference.

One non-voter told me he didn't vote because politicians "are all the same. Just pigs at the trough."

That one hurt.

Nevertheless, we have to ensure that our democracy provides legitimate government for all of its citizens—even reluctant voters.

In a democracy, voting is an essential democratic right. When I was campaigning and asked older voters if they were going to vote, the answer was often, "I fought for the right to vote; you bet I'm going to" or, "Of course! My father fought in the war and insisted that I vote in every election." In 2019, I took my mother, who was eighty-six, to the polling station to vote.

"I've voted in every election since 1954," she said as we were coming out. I was struck by how important it was for her to vote.

But it's easy for some people to take voting for granted. Sharmarke Dubow's story might help non-voters appreciate the privilege they have.

In the fall of 2015, Sharmarke Dubow and I were canvassing in Victoria on a Sunday. Dubow was a newcomer to Canada and was one of my loyal volunteers. He had been born in Somalia and had

Jo-Ann Roberts, as interim leader of the Green Party of Canada, attends a Remembrance Day ceremony with her mother in Halifax, NS, on November 11, 2019. [KEN KELLY]

come to Canada as a refugee. When I met him, he was a permanent resident but did not yet have citizenship. His immigration status was one of the reasons he wanted to work on my campaign. In 2014, the Harper government had passed legislation to make it harder to qualify for citizenship. The residency requirement changed from having to have lived in Canada three out of four years after becoming a permanent resident to four out of six years. Dubow had just met the three-year criteria when the law changed. It meant he had to wait an extra year to become a citizen and couldn't vote in the 2015 election. He was very disappointed and upset with the Harper government.

We went door to door in a subsidized housing complex of two-storey brick townhouses on Blanshard Street across from a shopping mall. The traffic was whizzing by, but we could still hear kids playing on the playground at the centre of the complex.

Dubow has an engaging smile and a demeanour that radiates warmth. We met a lot of newcomers as we knocked on doors— many who wouldn't have opened their doors if I hadn't been with him. He was able to get conversations started to find out whether they could or would vote. Many who could vote said they were planning to do so, but they hadn't seen any other candidates and weren't sure if they were registered. We took the time to ensure they had what they needed to make voting possible. It was slow going, but highly productive.

Finally, I said to Dubow, "Let's take a break and sit on a bench at the playground." As we sat, I asked him why he was willing to spend every Sunday knocking on doors with me after working all week. "You're one of my best volunteers," I said, "but you can't even vote."

"Jo-Ann," he said, "I have seen people killed because they were fighting for the right to vote. I want every Canadian to know they can cast a ballot and should never take that right for granted." He said he knew personally how much government policy could affect a person's life. "Ask any refugee. The government holds our lives in its hands—voting matters. Many Canadians who were born and brought up here have forgotten that."

There's a follow-up to this story: in 2018, a year after becoming a Canadian citizen, Dubow voted for the first time. He subsequently ran for and won a city council seat in Victoria, BC. He was the first Somali-born Canadian elected to a city council in Canada and the first Black city councillor in Victoria in 152 years.

I often think of Dubow when someone tells me they don't vote. Do they know what power they have? Do they think about it as a duty to democracy and civil society, or have we lost sight of those concepts?

Sadly, it is unlikely we will see a political promise to introduce compulsory voting in Canada in the near future. The backlash from the vaccination mandates that were introduced during the COVID-19 pandemic has created a political climate in Canada where anything that could be seen as a challenge to personal freedom is a red flag, and the major political parties see no value in changing the status quo.

If nothing changes, voter turnout will continue to decline, even though 74 percent of Canadians believe voting is a civic duty. The big question is whether the duty associated with the right to vote should be enforced by law.

Either way, we must find a way to get people out to the polls again—before voter turnout drops to a point where the results are no longer legitimate and our democracy becomes vulnerable to authoritarian forms of government.

Three generations meet a national icon—and a believer in the importance of electoral reform—in Vancouver, BC, September 28, 2018. From L: Jo-Ann Roberts, her daughter Alyson Kelly (holding her niece Georgia), and Dr. David Suzuki. [KEN KELLY]

CHAPTER 10

KICK-STARTING A VOTING REVOLUTION

20 Practical Tips

AFTER WORKING AS A REPORTER FOR FORTY YEARS, I thought I knew how politics worked in this country. I went into the 2015 federal election as a candidate confident that all I had to do was convince people I was the best person for the job, and they would vote for me.

I quickly learned that isn't how it works.

In the process, I discovered that there was so much we don't know about how and why our electoral system is set up the way it is. It has functioned for over a century with minor changes along the way, but it is now on the verge of losing a whole generation of voters. It is vulnerable to outside interference and manipulation by interest groups and is losing the confidence of the people it was established to serve.

We need a voting revolution—a non-violent but powerful movement to insist that the right to vote—the very core activity of our democracy—is reinvigorated, restored, and respected.

The drop in voter turnout is a symptom of a more serious illness. Is it apathy or ignorance or frustration? Probably all of the above. I wrote this book because I don't think those in power are interested in solving this problem.

Organizations like Fair Vote Canada and Apathy is Boring have made some difference in voter turnout. Elections Canada and provincial elections institutions are trying, but their hands are largely tied; after all, they report to their respective governments. Electoral bodies can make recommendations, though, and are doing their best to make voting fair, safe, and accessible. Elections Canada and its provincial counterparts are committed to ensuring citizens know how and where to vote.

So here's my final practical suggestion: it is time to add responsibility for voter turnout to Elections Canada and the provincial and territorial elections bodies.

VOTING REVOLUTION TIP

Call for Elections Canada and the provincial and territorial elections bodies to take responsibility for voter turnout. Give Elections Canada and its provincial counterparts the power and mandate to promote voting.

Throughout this book, I've offered a number of concrete tips listing steps both individual Canadians and the Canadian government and electoral bodies can take to kick-start a voting revolution. For the record, let's recap:

1. Avoid the trap of strategic voting. Vote for the candidate you consider the best representative of your riding.

2. When considering polling results, ask yourself: Do these results disclose the details of how the poll was done, who conducted it, when and where it was done, the sample size, and the margin of error, and do they say where I can get a copy of the entire survey?

3. Encourage Elections Canada to limit the margin of error of polls that can be released during a campaign period and revise its regulations so media outlets cannot publish poll results when the margin of error exceeds a particular number (such as ± 5).

4. Call for fixed, stable funding for public broadcasting in Canada. A free press and public broadcasting are essential to a functional democracy. Voters can help by advocating for funding that is at arm's-length from partisan political and commercial interests and supported by a tax on other media platforms.

5. Work toward proportional representation: collectively agree to try some form of electoral reform in the next election cycle, and hold a federal referendum on electoral reform. If a majority favours PR, have a Citizens' Assembly recommend a system; hold at least one election under that system. Follow up with another referendum to determine whether voters want to keep that system.

6. Advocate to lower the voting age to sixteen and make civics education about elections and democracy mandatory in schools. We've already lowered the age from

twenty-one to eighteen; we can take the next step. Also: promise to raise voters and talk about politics in a civilized manner!

7.   Advocate for Canada to impose consequences, enforced through the Elections Act, when parties create untrue, deceptive, or destructive campaign narratives.

8.   Encourage Elections Canada to experiment with taking the political party name off the ballot to encourage voters to elect a specific candidate rather than to blindly vote for a party. This would make local candidates more accountable to constituents during a campaign.

9.   Persuade government to bring back the per-vote subsidy. This is the single most significant change we can make to election financing and the simplest way, barring proportional representation, to make every vote matter and let the public know their vote has value.

10.   Have government introduce a monthly income-replacement allowance for political candidates. This would level the playing field and make becoming a candidate accessible to a more diverse range of people.

11.   Advocate for fixed election dates that are truly fixed, with strict criteria for not adhering to them. Allow a governing party to adjust election dates only with a valid reason that is supported by other parties. Alternatively, require a specific amount of notice—sixty or ninety days—to call an early election.

12. Actively support mandatory voting because it would eliminate the need for political parties to spend time and money on GOTV campaigns and because having more people vote increases the democratic legitimacy of the mandate given to those who are elected. It would also reduce the power inequity between those who typically vote and those who don't.

13. Call for Elections Canada and the provincial and territorial elections bodies to take responsibility for voter turnout. Give Elections Canada and its provincial counterparts the power and mandate to promote voting.

These are concrete, achievable goals. But they're not the only practical steps Canadian governments and electoral regulators can take. Here are some further suggestions that can help turn back the tide of declining voter numbers:

14. Hold elections on Saturdays and make the day a national/provincial holiday.

15. Offer an incentive for voting by giving everyone the day off—the whole day, not just a few hours. According to the Canada Elections Act, eligible voters must currently have three consecutive hours to exercise their right to vote on a federal election day, but it is up to the employer to meet this requirement, and employees aren't always aware of their rights—or may not be willing to risk pushing the issue with their boss. A mandatory day off would solve this problem.

16. Provide free public transportation on voting day and fund groups to offer a meal to anyone with proof of voting. This would make going to the polls an enjoyable community activity.

17. Allow voter information stations near polling places.

18. Offer a tax credit for voting.

19. Provide a one-day voucher for admission to a National Park to everyone who votes. It adds value to the concept of voting and sends the message that the government wants you to vote.

20. Create legislation that says if voter turnout falls below 50 percent, an election is no longer valid and must be held again. At the very least, this would give political parties a vested interest in increasing voter turnout.

Is it enough to just concentrate on voting? Friends have told me, "It's only one element of our democracy," and they're right. Our democratic system also includes freedom of thought, belief, opinion, and expression; freedom of the press and other media communication; freedom of peaceful assembly; freedom of association; and freedom of conscience and religion. These freedoms are all essential to democracy and they must be protected at all costs.

I believe the best way to protect all these freedoms is through the ballot box. If we voluntarily give up our right to vote, then these other freedoms are not safe.

It's time for the voting revolution to begin.

ACKNOWLEDGEMENTS

WHEN I LOST THE 2015 ELECTION I WAS DEVASTATED. I thought my political life was over. Little did I know it was just beginning. One of the things that motivated me to get up during those horrible days was the idea that I should write an essay to enter the Dalton Camp Award. It's a contest with a $10,000 prize for the best essay on the link between media and democracy. My entry didn't win, but the exercise helped me realize that I had learned things in the 2015 campaign that might make a book someday. Some of what appears in Chapter 1 was in that essay.

It took a lot of people and experiences to get me from that point to this one. I was inspired by Moira Dann and Gregor Craigie to apply for the MFA in Creative Nonfiction at the University of King's College in Halifax. Being accepted in the program made all the difference to this book. Lezlie Lowe was my first-year mentor; she helped me find both the story and my voice and helped me make the shift from radio writer to creative non-fiction writer. What a woman! To Rachel Ganz and Dorothy Wigmore, my writing buddies, thanks for being kind and gentle critics and friends forever. In my second year, I had the incredible Ken McGoogan as my mentor—lucky me. He challenged my ideas and then cheered me on to the finish line. He also got me through a broken ankle and several life crises, going over and above the call of duty. Finally, to round out the King's crowd, Stephen Kimber bought me a beer and convinced me not to quit, Dean Jobb helped me take researching to a whole new level, and I was so determined to impress the amazing Kim Pittaway that I learned how to rewrite until I got it right. I also had a dream of someday having my book for sale in the King's Co-op Bookstore. Thank you, Paul MacKay.

On a political level, thank you to Elizabeth May, Stefan Jonsson, and Sonia Theroux for asking me to be a candidate and taking care of me while I found my way. Greens in Ottawa, especially Debra Eindiguer and Honora Nedwidek, and in British Columbia, PEI, Ontario, Nova Scotia, and New Brunswick, you are all part of this story. I hope you know who you are. To my friends Dennis and Gwen Anholt, thanks for making sure I had a regular dose of Liberal opinions to consider. And to Gordon and Theresa Phillips, thank you for your hospitality and prayers.

I know now why so many writers thank their editors. How does anyone finish a book without one? Angela Mombourquette agreed to see me, based on a cheeky email. I loved her immediately and wept when she said she would make the case for my book to the team at Nimbus. Angela gets me. She makes me the absolute best version of my writing self. I hope there are many more coffee dates in our future. To Whitney Moran and everyone at Nimbus, thank you for taking a chance on me and believing we should talk about democracy now, more than ever. I feel like I have joined a family. I wouldn't be at Nimbus if it hadn't been for Carol Bruneau, a writer I have admired for a decade. We are both readers at the same church.

I started sitting in her pew on Sundays. (Yes, Carol, it was on purpose!) She listened to my tales of woe when I was worrying about finding either an agent or a publisher. Carol urged me to keep trying Nimbus; she felt it would be a good fit. Her encouragement helped me overcome my anxiety. Carol, you were an answer to my prayer.

On a personal level, my mom always believed I could and should do this. Thank you for your love, and for paying my tuition second semester. Also, a big hug for hanging on to my grade 6 notebook and grade 7 speech, which were invaluable to me. To my children—Chris, Claire, Aly, and Meg—you were brave enough to allow me to interview all four of you and then trust I would get it right. I was a bit surprised how shocked you were that it was correct and interesting!

To my sister Jane, thanks for always providing a quiet place to write when I needed it. And to my sister Laurie and brother, David, you keep me humble and make me laugh.

I have too many friends to thank individually, but a couple must be mentioned. Brenda Betts, when I felt the deadlines were overwhelming you helped me set my own deadlines and then annoyingly asked daily if I'd met them. Trips to Mission Mart were always my reward. Every writer needs a friend like you. And Sister Joyce Harris, our monthly check-ins were fuel for my writer's soul.

Finally, my love, the guy who brings me coffee in bed every morning, Ken. You have been at sign-waves and debates, celebrated my wins and dried my tears when I lost so many times. This book was my dream, and you sacrificed to make it a reality. I couldn't have done it without you.

I despair over those who have given up and have decided not to vote. I have written this book to try and address that, but I have hope for the future of democracy because of those who still vote, and I owe an immense debt of gratitude to those who took a leap of faith and voted for me in two provinces and four elections. Thank you. Your courage and your belief in democracy fuels my drive to start a voting revolution.

SELECTED BIBLIOGRAPHY

Gutstein, Donald. *Not A Conspiracy Theory: How Business Propaganda Hijacks Democracy*. Toronto: Key Porter Books, 2009.

Internet Archive, "Canada Unity Memorandum of Understanding (Freedom Convoy 2022)." December 3, 2021. archive.org/details/convoymou2022/mode/2up.

Marland. Alex. *Whipped: Party Discipline in Canada*. Vancouver: UBC Press, 2020.

Marland, Alex and Thierry Giasson, eds. *Inside the Campaign: Managing Elections in Canada*. Vancouver: UBC Press, 2020.

May, Elizabeth. *Losing Confidence: Power, Politics and the Crisis in Canadian Democracy*. Toronto: McClelland and Stewart, 2009.

May, Elizabeth. *Who We Are: Reflections on my Life and Canada*. Vancouver: Greystone Books, 2014.

Meslin, Dave. *Teardown: Rebuilding Democracy from the Ground Up*. Toronto: Penguin Canada, 2019.

Monbiot, George. *Out of the Wreckage: A New Politics for An Age of Crisis*. London: Verso Books, 2017.

Moscrop, David. *Too Dumb for Democracy? Why We Make Bad Political Decisions and How We Can Make Better Ones.* Fredericton: Goose Lane Editions, 2019.

Nash, Peggy. *Women Winning Office: An Activist's Guide to Getting Elected.* Tkaronto: Between the Lines, 2022.

Savoie, Donald. *Democracy in Canada: The Disintegration of Our Institutions.* Montreal and Kingston: McGill-Queen's University Press, 2019.

Special Committee on Electoral Reform. *Strengthening Democracy in Canada: Principles, Process and Public Engagement for Electoral Reform.* Ottawa: House of Commons, December 2016.

Statistics Canada. "Civic Engagement and Political Participation in Canada." www150.statcan.gc.ca/n1/pub/89-652-x/89-652-x2015006-eng.htm#a6.

YouTube. "Conservative Leader Pierre Poilievre on Federal Govt.'s New Affordability Measures." youtube.com/watch?v=X_-ZQ5BHom4.

Jo-Ann Roberts is an award-winning journalist who is passionate about democracy, public broadcasting, and fighting climate change. She spent twenty years as a CBC Radio host and covered more elections than she can count. She is the former interim leader of the Green Party of Canada and has been a candidate in four elections—a runner-up, but never the winner. She has an MFA in Creative Nonfiction from the University of King's College.